Plays for Children

Helen Rose worked for several years as Assistant Editor on the Theatre Desk at *Time Out* magazine before becoming a freelance journalist. She is currently a freelance editor and upholsterer and lives in London with her two sons, Finn and Lorcan.

D0683378

Plays for Children

Indigo Mill
by Nick Fisher

Body Talk
by Andy Rashleigh

Odessa and the Magic Goat
by John Agard

Little Victories
by Shaun Prendergast

Selected with an introduction
by Helen Rose

faber and faber

First published in 2000
by Faber and Faber Limited
3 Queen Square, London WC1N 3AU

Typeset by Faber and Faber Ltd
Printed in England by Mackays of Chatham plc, Chatham, Kent

All rights reserved
Introduction © Helen Rose, 2000
Indigo Mill © Nick Fisher, 2000
Body Talk © Andy Rashleigh, 2000
Odessa and the Magic Goat © John Agard, 2000
Little Victories © Shaun Prendergast, 1994

Little Victories was first published by Samuel French Ltd in 1994

Nick Fisher, Andy Rashleigh, John Agard and Shaun Prendergast
are hereby identified as authors of their work in accordance with Section 77
of the Copyright, Designs and Patents Act 1988

*This book is sold subject to the condition that it shall not,
by way of trade or otherwise, be lent, resold, hired out
or otherwise circulated without the publisher's prior consent
in any form of binding or cover other than that in which
it is published and without a similar condition including
this condition being imposed on the subsequent purchaser*

A CIP record for this book is available from the British Library

ISBN 0-571-20339-6

2 4 6 8 10 9 7 5 3 1

Contents

All professional and amateur rights in these plays are strictly reserved and applications for permission to perform them must be made in advance, before rehearsals begin.

For *Indigo Mill* apply to International Artistes, Mezzanine Floor, 235 Regent Street, London W1R 8AX. The original music for *Indigo Mill* by Andrew Dodge can also be obtained from International Artistes.

For *Body Talk* apply to Andrew Mann Ltd, 1 Old Compton Street, London W1V 5PS.

For *Odessa and the Magic Goat* apply to Caroline Sheldon Literary Agency, Thorley Manor Farm, Thorley, Yarmouth PO41 0SJ.

For *Little Victories,* professional enquiries, apply to M. Steinberg Playwrights, 409 Triumph House, 187–191 Regent Street, London W1R 7WT. For amateur enquiries, please apply to Samuel French Ltd, 52 Fitzroy Street, London W1P 6JR.

No performance may be given unless a licence has first been obtained.

Biographical Notes on the Authors

Nick Fisher has written over twenty stage plays, including six specifically for younger audiences. *Indigo Mill* (Polka Theatre, London, 1992) was one of *Time Out*'s Four Best Children's Plays of the Year. In 1995 Nick was an Arts Council writer-in-residence with Action Transport Theatre for Young People. In 1990 his community play *The Best Years* was commissioned by the ILEA to mark the final days of the Authority and played at the Bloomsbury Theatre. His plays for adult audiences have been premièred at major theatres around Britain and abroad. Nick has also written twenty plays and six serials for radio. His play *Vox Humana* received a Special Commendation from the jury at the 1997 Prix Europa Awards. Nick has recently written his first feature film, The *Clock*, to be directed by George Sluizer.

Andy Rashleigh was writer-in-residence at The Unicorn Theatre for Children from 1992 to 1996; his other plays there include *Now and Then* and *Shakespeare's Apprentice*. As well as these, Andy has written many other plays for children and adults over the past twenty years.

John Agard is one of the most popular children's poets writing in Britain today. He has published numerous books of poetry for children as well as for adults. His latest collection of poetry for young children, *We Animals Would Like a Word With You*, won a Smarties Award. He has written several plays for children for the Little Angel Marionette Theatre. In 1998 he was appointed the first poet-in-residence at the BBC.

Shaun Prendergast began his career while studying at Bretton Hall. His first play, *Potters Wheel*, won five awards at the 1980 National Student Drama Festival, including Best New Play. *Little Victories* was jointly commissioned by Trestle and Quicksilver Theatre Companies and won the *Time Out* Best Children's Play Award. He has also written an award-winning children's BBC Drama radio series, *Travelling Light*. He now divides his time between acting and increasingly writing for television, film, stage and radio.

Introduction

Why take children to the theatre? What's the point? They have television, videos, computers and all sorts of stimulation at home and in school. Magic – that's why. Good theatre is magical.

Good theatre keeps the audience totally engaged; it springs off the stage, it is immediate and unpredictable, it questions and it answers back – it is alive and vital in an age where so much of our leisure time is spent in the solitary pursuit of something the other side of a screen. Children love and crave the two-way nature of theatre because it involves them in something real, and however much of a fantasy they may be being drawn into on stage, the actors weaving that fantasy are living beings and this casts a spell of its own. Children today casually accept as normal all sorts of technological wizardry, growing up with computer graphics and the sort of virtual reality games that leave me awe-struck, and yet these same children can still be enchanted by a piece of theatre. An audience that is touched by the magic of a production will be so involved with the action on stage that the interval lights are a disappointing surprise rather than an opportunity for an ice-cream, and it gives me a thrill to watch children enraptured by this ancient art and to know that the magic doesn't die.

How many adults, unless they are parents, even know that children's theatre exists? In spite of being a theatre critic for many years, I had no idea of the enormous range and excellence of writing being produced in children's theatre. Like most adults, until I had children of my own I had no reason to go to children's theatre and had a vague concept of it probably being something to do with puppets or involving lots of slapstick and audience participation.

I really was not prepared for the innovation, the styles of writing, the range of topics, the bravery and audacity of some of the work I saw. There were pieces which *I* found challenging, which tackled issues I imagined would be far too complex for children to appreciate, and yet here were companies pushing the limits, not just of their own art, but of our expectations of children's ability to understand what was being presented.

Children are like sponges, they absorb things through the pores of their skin, they are intuitive and very receptive. It is generally accepted that children are easier to hypnotize than adults because they have such open imaginations, they are willing and enthusiastic in their suspension of disbelief. Good playwrights understand this: they know that once you have them hooked and on your imaginative wavelength, you can take children anywhere. The trick, of course, is to keep them hooked, and if anyone thinks that writing for children is a piece of cake they should sit in an audience of bored and restive children and see how they behave when the play is failing to keep them engaged. This makes children the most demanding of audiences to write for and only the very brave and the very talented take on this challenge and make a success of it.

This selection of plays brings together four very different works, but each has that very special quality which holds the audience's attention and draws it into the web of words and wonder.

These plays represent among the best in original children's theatre. There are many fine examples of adaptations, and I know that theatre companies sometimes favour them simply because it is easier for them to market an adaptation of a famous book or story than an original work and, at the end of the day, they have to get bums on seats just to stay afloat. A great number of companies manage to do both: balancing in their scheduling the almost guaranteed success of some good quality adaptations with the inevitable risk of an original piece. In all the financial juggling theatre companies have to do they find themselves obliged to produce work that can be dove-tailed to topics on the National Curriculum; they are made to jump through all sorts of hoops just to get the funding and support to continue. Schools cannot realistically afford theatre visits which are seen to be just for 'fun'; they have tight budgets too, so in order to justify a theatre visit they also look for plays which can be financed out of a specific curriculum budget. However, out of all these constraints there arise memorable and challenging plays which leave all these issues behind and soar into another world, taking their audience with them. It is thanks to Artistic Directors of vision, enterprise and sheer guts that we have the quality of work in this volume.

The whole of Britain is scattered with touring children's theatre companies (listed at the back of this volume), but there are only two building-based companies – the Polka Theatre in Wimbledon (the *only* purpose-built children's theatre in Britain) and the Unicorn (now located in North London after moving from its shared venue in the West End of London) – and yet in spite of, or perhaps because of, the itinerant nature of British children's theatre, there is a great, moving body of innovative, exciting, uplifting work to be found throughout the country.

This selection is important because I want to show the wealth, breadth and excellence of original work being produced. In this volume only four plays, commissioned by four very different theatre companies, are represented. They are wonderful and very special plays, but they do not stand alone – they are backed up by a great bank of other plays and other companies producing excellent work.

On show here is a range of styles and subjects; whether it be John Agard's beautifully lyrical Caribbean poem for the Little Angel Marionette Theatre, *Odessa and the Magic Goat*, or Andy Rashleigh's hilarious biology lesson, *Body Talk*; the historical fiction around the life and work of William Morris in *Indigo Mill*, or the poignant, but life-affirming, story of childhood death in Shaun Prendergast's brave *Little Victories*, I believe these to be plays to savour as well as to study, plays that show us how exciting, varied and, yes, educational, theatre can be.

This is what I want to share – the magic of children's theatre. Read them, study them, dissect them for the Literacy Hour, but above all enjoy them: if they touch a chord on the page, just imagine how powerful they are on the stage.

Helen Rose
November 1999

INDIGO MILL

Nick Fisher

For Hedda and Tom

Indigo Mill was first performed at the Polka Theatre, London, on 30 April 1992 with the following cast:

Hope Sally Ann Matthews
Stella Jo-Anne Knowles
William Morris Nigel Bowden
Jack/Fortune Doug Smith
Jane Morris Olivia Carruthers
Wardle/Stitchit Christopher Robbie

Directed by Caroline Smith
Designed by Helen Skillicorn
Lighting designed by Neil Fraser
Stage managed by Andrew Wiltshire
Lyrics by Nick Fisher
Music composed by Andrew Dodge

Characters

Hope
Stella
William Morris
Jane Morris
Jack
Thomas Wardle
John Fortune
Stitchit
Man on Street
Woman on Street
Waitress
Old Man
Scruffy Woman
Joe

*This play can be performed by a minimum cast of six,
doubling as follows:*

Actress 1 Hope
Actress 2 Stella/Waitress
Actress 3 Jane/Woman on Street/Scruffy Woman

Actor 1 William Morris
Actor 2 Fortune/Jack
Actor 3 Wardle/Stitchit/Old Man/Joe/Man on Street

*The action of the play begins in 1880.
It is mainly set in Clerkenwell, in Hammersmith and at
Merton Abbey Mills.*

Act One

Music – 'stitching theme'. An East End sweatshop; a setting of grey, black and white except for two finished dresses on dummies. Hope and Stella work with needle and thread. Stitchit enters.

Stitchit Not finished? Not yet finished?

Hope (*indicating dresses*) Those are.

Stitchit I'm not concerned with those. I'm concerned with these.

Hope But there's so much to do.

Stitchit Of course. This is a busy time. So things need to be finished – quickly.

Hope You can't stitch quick when you get cramp in your fingers.

Stitchit Then un-get it.

Stella And it's hard to work when the light's so bad.

Stitchit Hard? Hard is the life I saved you from. A pair of orphans – no food in your bellies, no roof over your heads. When you were so young you can't even remember. Out of the goodness of my heart I take you in. All I ask in return is a bit of stitching, an elegance of sewing, a cascade of pretty needlework. And all you can say is – 'it's hard'?

Hope But with Stella's eyes so bad, it *is* hard. If you made this place brighter and lighter, you'd soon see a difference.

Stitchit Brighter? Lighter? This is no playground – this is a place of work.

Hope But why so much, so quick?

Stitchit Because of Ascot.

Hope What's Ascot?

Stitchit Why, it is the horse-racing. It is the countryside. Where the fine ladies wear their fine dresses. Their fine new dresses that you are making . . . far too slowly. Back to work!

He leaves.

Song – Stitching (Hope and Stella).

Stitching – stitching
Every day and night
We hem a dress
We have no light
We get no rest
From all our stitching – stitching

Needles in and out
And up and down
And round about
And round and round
We go on stitching – stitching

Fingers feeling dead
We work grey thread
Should be in bed
With eyes so red
From all this stitching – stitching

Oh we're itching to be switching from this
    stitching
Yes, we're itching, fingers twitching, to be pitching

Out this stitching, which in truth is unenriching
Stupid stitching!

Stella I can hardly see what I'm doing, Hope.

Hope Rest your eyes. Don't worry – I'll spot Stitchit if he's coming back.

Stella Horse-racing. In the countryside. Wouldn't that be grand.

Hope Wouldn't it just.

Stella Fresh air. Sunshine. These grey walls and this grey city is all I've ever known. Do you have any memories of anything else?

Hope No. (*Pause.*) Except – there is one thing. But I'm not sure if it's a memory, or a dream, or a nothing at all really.

Stella Tell me about it.

Hope Well, it starts with a sound.

Music begins, low and mysterious.

Then there's a colour.

Blue light.

A pattern.

Blue light now rippling.

And something moving, turning.

A shadowy circular movement.

Then a figure appears – a man.

A figure in silhouette.

And there's a voice.

A voice echoes over the music repeating the word 'more'. But suddenly the music ends, the vision disappears and all that is left is the cold, grey sweatshop as before.

Stella And?

Hope And it always disappears when I want to know more.

Stella What do you think it means?

Hope I don't know. But it might be something important about my past. Like the lost thread of my life. How I'd love to stitch that in place. Quick – Stitchit's coming!

They dive back to work. Stitchit and Fortune enter.

Stitchit You may stop work. This is Mr John Fortune – the new owner of these premises.

Fortune Hard at work, girls? Excellent. Every stitch counts.

Stitchit This is Miss Sarah Bradley's dress. And this will be for Lady Markham.

Fortune Very fine. There will be a bonus coming to you for this, Mr Stitchit.

Hope What? We did the work!

Fortune I beg your pardon?

Hope We did all that. Why don't *we* get a bonus?

Stitchit I'm dreadfully sorry, Mr Fortune . . .

Fortune No, no. Perhaps the little imp has a point. How many more dresses are there to complete?

Stitchit Seven.

Fortune Then you girls will be working through the night and past the dawn. But if you finish everything to Mr Stitchit's absolute satisfaction, you may share a quarter of a pound of Mayfair bon-bons. Now – the order books.

Fortune and Stitchit leave.

Hope (*witheringly*) A quarter of a pound of bon-bons! I'm going to Ascot. Want to come?

Stella We can't go to Ascot.

Hope Yes we can – here and now. And I'm not going as Hope but as Lady Whatsit. (*She takes a dress from its dummy. Posh voice*) My dear – would you help me into my new dress?

Stella Hope – put it back. You can't touch that.

Hope Why not? Er . . . (*posh voice*) I cannot touch my own dress? Do not be so ridiculous. (*She puts it on.*) My, my – it is on the large side. I dare say the terrible imps who made it are to blame. Perhaps this will help it to fit properly . . . (*She fills out the bust with some spare material.*)

Stella Oh, Hope – you do look funny.

Hope picks up a stick and improvises a parasol.

Hope Ah, my parasol. One must stay cool in society. And of course I need to wear my high heels to keep my dainty ankles above the mud.

She struts on tiptoe. Stella claps with delight.

I do like it here at Ascot. People of such quality to talk to. Why, I do believe that is Prince Charming. Hello, Prince!

And Stitchit enters.

Stitchit What is going on here? Take that off this instant!

Hope whips off the dress.

Stitchit This time you have gone too far.

Hope Only a bit of fun.

Stitchit Fun? Let's see how much fun you find back on the streets. Back where you belong – where your parents dumped you!

Hope Where what?

Stitchit They just threw you away – like the rubbish you are. Now get out of here. Go!

Hope Where to?

Stitchit That's your problem – not mine. Well, if you won't go, I'll make you.

Hope clings to Stella, but Stitchit drags her out.

Stella Hope! Hope!

Song – The Thread of Life (Stella).

Good luck Hope – Don't give up Hope
Grasp the thread of your life
Though you're out on the street again
Doubting we'll manage to meet again
Don't despair
Try to pick up the thread
Try to pick up your life
Try to pick up the stitch – take care
With the thread of your life – Hope

Stella leaves. On shadowy streets a woman begs.

Woman Spare some change, sir. Spare some change.

*A passing man looks the other way. The woman spits.
A rough-looking man enters. Hope enters and watches.*

Man How much you got then?

Woman Thruppence ha'penny.

Man What – all day?

Woman Yeah.

Man You're lying.

Woman I ain't. I've been asking till me throat's sore – and that's all I got.

Man Well, hand it over anyway.

Woman No. It's my turn to keep the earnings. We agreed.

Man I've changed my mind. So – give it here! (*He wrestles the money from her and begins to go.*)

Hope Hey – stop! I saw you!

Man Oh – saw me, did you? Saw me? Dear oh Lor – how frit I am. Trembling like a man on the scaffold. Grab her!

The woman grabs Hope.

Hope What are you doing?

Woman Grabbing you.

Hope I was trying to help. He attacked you.

Woman Simply a matrimonial disputation, dearie. He's my husband.

Man And who are you?

Hope Hope.

Man Some Hope! Hahaha. Got any money?

Hope I ain't got nothing.

Man You've got a coat. That's something. Something we might get a farthing for.

Woman He's right. Take it off, dearie.

Hope I'll freeze.

Man Not if you jump up and down a lot. Take it off!

Hope Won't.

Man Then we'll do it for you.

They pull at her coat. Jack enters carrying a stick.

Hope Leave me alone!

Jack Indeed. Do leave her alone – if you know what's good for you. If on the other hand, you'd like a chat with my friend Willow . . . (*lifting stick*) . . . carry on.

Woman Jack. We didn't mean no harm.

Jack I'm sure you didn't.

Man She's not a friend of yours, is she?

Jack I never set eyes on her in my life. But you know how I hate to see cruelty or injustice. Let her go.

Woman Times are awful bad, Jack. If we could just have her coat.

Jack (*icily dangerous*) I believe I said – let her go.

They release Hope, who moves towards Jack.

There – that wasn't so difficult, was it. Did they hurt you my dear?

Hope Not really, sir.

Jack Sir? Plain Jack will do. Jack o' the Night they sometimes call me – 'cos I never sleep. My eyes only close when I wink. (*to man and woman*) Still here? You must want a chat with Willow after all.

He moves towards them. They run. Jack laughs.

Cowards! You shouldn't be tangling with the likes of

them – they're a bad lot and no mistake. Now, what's your name?

Hope Hope.

Jack Now there's a pretty name. Full of prospects, that is. So, Hope – tell Jack o' the Night what you're doing on the streets of his patch at this hour.

Hope Nothing. I'm just passing through.

Jack But where are you going?

Hope shrugs and starts to leave.

Wait! Wouldn't you like a friend? A friend who can teach you some tricks?

Hope pauses. Jack shows empty hands then makes a handkerchief appear – as if from Hope's ear.

Hope How did you do that?

Jack Would you like to learn some tricks, Hope?

Hope Yeah.

Jack Then I'll teach you. 'Cos tricks are what you need in this cruel world. But first – are you hungry?

Hope Starving.

Jack Bellies always come first with Jack. And there's a nice stew on the stove just waiting to fill those bellies to the brim. Come on.

They leave. Scene changes to Clerkenwell Green. Thomas Wardle and William Morris sit at a table outside a coffee house. Jack enters and watches.

Waitress What would you like, gentlemen?

Morris Two coffees please.

Waitress Certainly, sir.

She leaves.

Wardle Clerkenwell Green. It is more like Clerkenwell Grey, is it not? Not a blade of grass to be seen.

Morris Yet this could still be a pleasant spot.

Wardle What? Close by some of the worst slums in the city?

Morris Do but use your imagination, Mr Wardle. Envisage change.

Wardle I cannot see how this will change. The people here are little better than animals.

Morris You describe only the surface. Underneath, everyone has an equal potential for goodness – and for change.

Wardle Poppycock. Some people are plain bad, Mr Morris. A thief is a thief – end of story.

The waitress returns with the coffees.

Waitress Two coffees. That'll be fourpence please.

Morris takes a note from a well-filled wallet.

Morris Can you change this? I fear I have nothing smaller.

Waitress That's alright, sir.

She takes the note and leaves.

Jack Well, Jack – you're in the right spot today and no mistake. (*He whistles.*) Hope?

Morris So where are the samples you purchased?

Wardle lifts a bag as Hope arrives beside Jack.

Hope Is it time for lunch? I'm hungry.

Jack Very shortly we'll have enough money to fill that belly of yours till it bursts. It's time to use one of the tricks I've taught you.

The waitress is bringing Morris his change.

See the gentleman receiving his change? He has a pocket-book full of money. He's clearly very rich.

Hope So he can let us have it – as we're very poor.

Jack (*nods*) Show me how well you've learned.

Hope creeps up behind Morris, who is examining some cloth samples.

Morris Well, if this is the best that chemical dyeing can achieve, there is still no competition for our natural dyes. So – difficult though it is, we will continue our experiments with indigo.

Hope deftly takes his wallet, but Wardle spots her.

Wardle (*grabbing her*) Hey – stop there!

Morris Mr Wardle, have you taken leave of your senses?

Wardle No, I have not. But this young pup has just made sure something took its leave of you. (*He prises the wallet from Hope's grasp.*)

Morris My pocket-book? But I never felt a thing.

Wardle It was neatly done. I would wager we have a seasoned criminal on our hands. We should find a constable.

Morris One moment. (*to Hope*) You are very quiet, my dear. You must know theft is a serious offence. The punishments are harsh. Tell me why you did it.

Hope 'Cos I ain't got nothing.

Wardle That is hardly a case to place before the magistrate.

Hope He's rich. We're poor. He can afford to let us have it. It's only fair.

Wardle I *will* find a constable.

Morris Hold a while, Mr Wardle. But a short time ago, you were saying how people cannot change – how a thief will always remain a thief. I maintain otherwise. I maintain that once placed in a beautiful, caring environment – like my own home, for instance – a thief can and will change.

Wardle I know your views. Oh, but you are not suggesting . . .?

Morris She would be the perfect subject to prove my argument.

Wardle She would *dis*prove it within the day.

Morris I think not.

Wardle You will regret this.

Morris I doubt it. (*to Hope*) My dear, I propose that you leave these grimy streets of the city for my home in Hammersmith.

Hope What if I don't want to come?

Morris You could choose a prison cell instead.

Hope Call that a choice?

Morris You will have to admit she is not stupid, Mr Wardle. Let us go.

Jack watches them leave.

Jack Damn and blast. She had skill that one. A touch as light as an angel's kiss. I'm not happy to see Hope disappear. No – I'm not happy about that, at all.

Jack leaves. Morris and Hope re-enter.

Morris Welcome to Hammersmith, Hope. Welcome to my home – to my creation. Do you like it?

During the following song, elements of Morris's design world/home appear, filling the previously dull stage with vibrant colour (elements such as iris, peony, etc., are all pre-1880 Morris designs).

Song – Inside Outside (Morris and Hope).

Hope
   Can I see more – Can I explore
   Can I examine each cupboard and drawer

Morris
   You can inspect – You can detect
   You can discover the things I collect
   But not in a drawer

   Step into my home – Step into my den
   Into my bower where outside is in
   Into a world where night becomes day
   Inside the outside where nature's the way

   Now here is an iris and here is a peony
   And here is acanthus and here anemone
   Here is a tulip and here a carnation
   A plucked pomegranate for Eden's creation

Hope
   Oh what a change – this is so strange
   Is this all magic – a spell you arrange

Morris
   This is all real – this you can feel

Yet it's illusion – there lies its appeal
So strong and so strange

Morris
A trailing of jasmine – A honeycomb climb

Hope/Morris
A peacock and dragon – A bluebell to chime

Morris/Hope
Here is some larkspur – Is this marigold

Morris
With that and with roses my garden takes hold

Step into creation – Step into my art
Into a voyage where nature's the chart

Both
We're inside the outside
Where trees are a shawl
We're inside the outside
Discovering all

*The stage is awash with colour by now – and Morris
has wrapped Hope in a beautiful shawl.*

Hope I've never seen nothing like this.

Morris Most of it I designed myself. With nature as my
guide.

Jane enters.

Jane William. You're back early.

Morris Hope, this is my wife, Jane. Hope has come to
stay with us.

Jane Really? And where has she come from?

Morris The streets of Clerkenwell. Where she tried to
steal my pocket-book.

Jane William, what do you think you're doing?

Morris Proving a point.

Jane Are you sure you're not simply making a mistake? (*to Hope*) What are you staring at?

Hope You. You're so beautiful.

Morris Yes – she is almost too beautiful, is she not? I will have the back bedroom prepared.

He leaves.

Hope That's a lovely necklace. What is it?

Jane (*warily*) Amber. From the Far East.

Hope You must be very rich.

Jane Not really. Though William does have some family money.

Hope He said he designs things. What do you do?

Jane Embroidery.

She shows Hope a half-finished piece.

Hope Is that all?

Jane I beg your pardon?

Hope I can do that.

Hope takes the embroidery. Music – 'stitching' theme – and lighting suggest time passing as she works. Morris enters and looks at the finished piece.

Morris You did this?

Hope I ain't done nothing wrong.

Morris No – aside from some remarkable mutilation of English grammar – you ain't done nothing wrong at all.

(*to Jane*) I thought I was befriending a waif – not a skilled worker.

Hope I'm not completely useless, you know. Where'd you buy all these colours?

Morris (*affronted*) Buy?

Jane Careful, Hope – creating colour is William's overriding passion.

Hope You make colour?

Morris I do my best. I have developed some excellent recipes for natural dyes – so much superior to chemical ones.

Jane So much more difficult to achieve though.

Morris True. Take indigo, Hope. From that comes the finest natural blue there is. But dyeing complex patterns with it is a nightmare. What with the bleaching and then the mordants needed for the adjective dyes, you can imagine.

Hope (*to Jane*) This *is* a house?

Jane What else would it be?

Hope Sounds like a school with him wittering on like that.

Morris Wittering on?

Jane You can be a little schoolmasterly at times.

Morris Oh, can I indeed?

Jane And quick to anger.

Morris I am not quick to anger!

Jane (*smiling*) I am sure Hope will be thrilled to learn more about dyeing.

Morris It's so exciting, Hope. I've gone back to medieval ways of making dyes – using herbs, roots and plants to create hundreds of different shades. I've discovered that kermes as well as cochineal and madder produces the most fabulous red . . .

Jane I think you're going a bit too fast, dear.

Morris What?

Jane Hope probably doesn't know what kermes, cochineal and madder are.

Morris Of course she does. (*to Hope*) Madder means something to you, doesn't it.

Hope Yeah.

Morris (*to Jane*) You see.

Hope It's when someone's a bit strange. Then they're madder than what you are, aren't they?

Jane smiles at Morris.

Morris Madder is also the name of a plant, Hope. Its root – crushed and mixed with liquid – makes a beautiful red dye. Wait . . . (*He rushes out.*)

Hope He's a bit like a child, ain't he.

Jane That's very clever of you. Yes – despite his years, he *is* like a child at times.

Hope Has he always done this dyeing and designing?

Jane No. At university he thought he would be a clergyman. Then he changed his mind and thought he'd be an architect. Then he changed his mind again and thought he'd be a poet. Then he changed his mind *again* and thought he'd be a stained-glass designer. Finally, he changed his mind one last time and decided he'd do more or less everything – all at once.

Hope Sounds like ten different people.

Morris rushes back with some boxes.

Morris Here are some of the raw materials. Look – madder. Isn't it exciting.

Hope (*holding root, unimpressed*) Not very.

Morris But changing it – that's where the excitement lies. Producing from that a red that will burn like the coals of hell itself. You can make red from this too.

He gives Hope a box. She puts her hand in.

Hope Ugh! What's this?

Morris Kermes. An insect.

Hope You might've said. I thought it was all roots and plants.

Morris We must take our inspiration from all aspects of the natural world. My designs stem from natural images. Likewise, my colours must come from natural sources.

During the following song colours are produced – pouring powders into liquids – to match the text.

Song – Madder (Morris, Jane, Hope).

Morris
  Brown you get from walnut husk
  So go scrumping after dusk
  Take them from your neighbour's tree
  Eat the insides for your tea

  Green is indigo with oak
  Fix it fast with a nice long soak
  Orange is weld and cochineal
  How those bright insects appeal

Morris/Jane
But to get ahead with a red get madder
You won't be sadder, you'll be flabber-
Gasted but gladder than an adder up a ladder
If you add a dab o' madder madder madder!

Morris
Black is woad with walnut root
Darker than the devil's suit
Indigo, kermes – purple chums
Brighter than Victoria plums

Yellow comes from weld or bark
Find that in your local park
Blue is indigo or woad
Both are things that can be . . .

Hope . . . growed!

All But to get ahead with a red . . . *etc.*

Hope is left alone, working on some cloth. Morris enters.

Morris What are you doing, Hope?

Hope (*shrugs*) Nothing.

Morris examines the cloth.

Morris Did you do this?

Hope What if I did?

Morris What have you been using – to make the dye?

Hope Just indigo. And some kermes and madder.

Morris This is darker than that would produce. This is like crushed mulberries. You've saddened it.

Hope Saddened?

Morris It means making the colour darker.

Hope Odd word for something that's just a bit of fun.

Morris Perhaps. But come now – tell me how you saddened the purple to this wonderful shade of claret.

Hope You won't be angry?

Morris Why should I be?

Hope I put some crushed walnut in.

Morris Walnut?

Hope I found it in your workshop. (*Pause.*) You're angry because I took it without asking.

Morris Hardly. I took it from my neighbour's tree without asking myself. Walnut. Of course. But how did you know?

Hope I just thought brown might work – if I could get it right.

Morris And you kept trying until you did? That is a lot of work, Hope.

Hope This ain't work.

Morris Well, no – it should be enjoyable too. As all work should be, one day. We need to change more than just colour in this world.

Hope This could be so much fun but . . . I don't ask for too much, do I?

Morris Not at all.

Hope Then can I ask for one thing? I want my friend back.

Morris Your friend?

Hope Stella. We used to work together in this horrible place on Saffron Hill.

Morris I will make some enquiries for you. (*He leaves.*)

Hope We could play with all these colours together, Stella. Imagine.

The low, mysterious music that accompanies her half-forgotten memory begins. Blue light. Rippling. Circular shadows. Voice calling 'more'. And a silhouetted figure advancing.

Who's there? Who are you?

Snap lighting change and music ends – it is Jack advancing, stick in hand. Hope screams. Jack disappears. Jane rushes in.

Jane Hope – what is it?

Hope I . . . there was this . . . I don't know.

Jane Did you fall asleep? Have you been having a nightmare?

Hope Yes – I must have been. I had this dream I often have. Only it turned into a horrible nightmare from somewhere else.

Jane You've been playing with the dyes when you should be asleep. You must be worn out. Now – off to bed with you.

Hope leaves. Lights fade – and come back on Morris, Wardle, Jane and Fortune. During this scene Hope enters and watches, unseen.

Wardle (*to Fortune*) Mr Morris's firm has had some financial difficulties. He is a very great artist – but the running of the business has been neglected.

Fortune And you believe I am the man to sort things out.

Wardle Well, you are a most successful businessman.

Fortune I have ways of getting results, it is true.

Morris As I have – in my art.

Fortune One needs to run a tighter ship in business, sir.

Morris There is nothing so rigorous as the creation of art.

Fortune Forgive me if I seemed to suggest otherwise. But precisely because you take that so seriously, you should not have to bother with the facts and figures of business. I could do that for you.

Jane That sounds very tempting, does it not?

Wardle And if the firm expands, you will reach a wider public.

Morris I would welcome that, it's true.

Fortune I have already drawn up an agreement for us to sign.

But as he hands Morris a document, Hope speaks.

Hope Don't sign nothing with him.

Morris Hope! What do you mean?

Hope He ain't someone you can trust.

Fortune I beg your pardon?

Wardle Please excuse this urchin, Mr Fortune. (*to Morris*) I told you no good would come of her. Underneath she clearly has not changed at all.

Jane Go to your room, Hope.

Hope No.

Morris You would disobey my wife?

Hope Yeah. To warn you against this penny-pinching

slave-driver. He owned that place where I used to work – sixteen hours a day, in bad light.

Morris Is this true, sir?

Fortune My affairs stretch far and wide. It is possible a business under my wing was being badly run by some unscrupulous employee. But I would never allow such things if they were brought to my personal attention.

Hope Wasn't it personal enough visiting the place? Offering us a few bon-bons if we slaved through the night?

Fortune I recognise you now. What is such a disreputable child doing here?

Hope Where's Stella?

Fortune Who?

Morris A young girl I have been endeavouring to trace. She also worked in that awful place on Saffron Hill – which is now boarded up. Why is that, sir?

Fortune I felt it was not making enough profit.

Morris What of those who worked there?

Fortune I had to let them go.

Jane You mean you put them on the streets?

Fortune That is the way of the world.

Morris (*coldly*) Thank you for sparing so much of your time. Unfortunately, an agreement between us will not be possible.

Wardle I beg you – reconsider. This is business.

Morris This, sir, is life! The door is that way.

Wardle I am sorry to see you so naive as to take the . . .

Morris Thank you and good day!

Wardle and Fortune leave.

Morris So much for securing the firm. But thank you, Hope.

Hope Stella's on the streets then. Don't suppose I'll ever see her again. (*She leaves.*)

Morris Poor child. But she is beginning to be a success here, is she not?

Jane Perhaps. Though you're still too trusting. You are such a dreamer, William.

Morris Looking at the realities of life around us, I would suggest the world could use a few dreams.

They leave. A sad, brief image of Hope working alone. Then lights up on Morris setting some stained glass. Jane enters.

Jane William – it is time we were getting ready.

Morris Mmm? For what?

Jane Lunch. With the Dearles.

Morris Oh yes – of course. Just two more minutes.

Jane Well, I shall start getting changed.

She leaves. Morris works. Suddenly Jane calls 'William, William' and rushes in with a jewellery box.

Morris What is it?

Jane My jewellery's been stolen. The amber necklace – everything.

Morris You mean someone has broken into the house?

Jane I don't think so. I just looked into Hope's room.

She's gone – and her bed hasn't been slept in.

Morris takes the box.

Morris My God. The smudges here – walnut and madder. The very dyes that Hope was working with.

Jane Then there can be no doubt. She hasn't changed. Hope is still a thief.

Interval.

Act Two

The sound of knives being sharpened. A shadowy setting of meat-hooks at Smithfield Market, with Hope and Jack – the latter with sword-stick in hand.

Song – Hanging by a Thread (Jack).

Jack

Do you know where you are?
I've brought you far, blindfolded and weeping
Smithfield Market for meat
Midnight's a treat, everyone sleeping

They'll think you stole those jewels
People are fools, Jack's mighty cunning
There's no chance of escape
It's much too late, don't you try running

Your life is hanging by a thread my dear
Hanging by a thread I fear
And if I cut that thread
Hope will be dead

Here's some lamb on a hook
Take a good long look, little Miss Clever
I could count you as sheep
Send you to sleep, now and forever

Here's a rabbit so still
And the rabbit ain't ill, it's fit – for eating
And if you try to hop
It's the angels up top you'll soon be greeting

Your life is hanging by a thread my dear
Hanging by a thread I fear
And if I cut that thread
You'll be like a carcass that's been bled:
For all the dark red blood
From your head will flood
'Till it fills the sluices with sticky juices
And the unruly life that you've led
Will have well and truly fled
And Hope – hanging by a thread from her head
Will be dead!

Hope Let me go. I've done nothing to you.

Jack And you've done nothing *for* me – yet. Except to open that jewellery box – at knife-point. Now, we've got work to do. (*He indicates a trap door.*) You first. Go on – down you go.

Hope What?

Jack It's the way into the sewers. And we need to travel underground.

Hope I don't want to go into the sewers.

Jack Would you rather swing from a hook? Go on!

They descend. Music. In the echoey sewers:

Hope It stinks.

Jack What were you expecting – French perfume?

Hope What if we get lost?

Jack I know where I'm going. And my lantern will guide the way. Now, take one of these. (*He gives her a pole.*)

Hope What's this?

Jack A tosher's pole. Push it through the sludge in front of you to feel the sewer floor – 'cos it ain't there in places. There's deep holes. If you fall in and go under, you're done for. Right – move!

They move forward. A loud swirling sound.

Hope What's that?

Jack Tide sweeping out down the main tunnel. We're safe – till it rises again. Then it'll fill every tunnel to the top. If we were still here, we'd drown for sure.

They move on. Hope screams.

Hope There's something in the water. I felt it against my leg.

Jack Whack your pole around a bit. It's a few rats, that's all.

Hope Rats?

Jack laughs as Hope beats about with her pole. They move on again.

Jack Not far now.

Hope Where are we?

Jack Near Hampstead. Which is where I want to be. No rats here.

Hope Why not?

Jack Even rats are frightened of this bit. They say there's dozens of wild boar – that bred in here.

Hope Wild boar? I might get killed. Let's go back.

Jack If you try and go back, you *will* get killed – by me.

They move on.

Stop. This is it. We're under the grounds of a big house,

full of valuable things. It's a well-guarded estate with a high wall. But there's a grill to the sewers – inside the grounds. There's a small gap that you can climb through. Then you can release the grill from above and let me up. Out you go.

Hope squeezes out.

Can you see the catches over the grill?

Hope Yeah.

Jack Undo them.

Hope No.

Jack Don't be silly now – do what I say.

Hope No, I won't.

Jack I'll kill you!

Hope How? You can't get me.

Jack I'll give you one more chance.

Hope Give a hundred – it'll make no difference.

Jack They'll put you in prison for stealing them jewels.

Hope They'll believe me.

Jack They don't believe people like you.

The swirling sound returns.

Oh no! Hope, let me out! The water's rising. It'll fill the tunnel to the top. If I stay here, I'll drown.

Hope Then you'd better go back – quick.

Jack Let me out!

Hope Goodbye, Jack.

Fade lights. Crescendo swirling and cries from Jack.

Then silence. Lights up on an old man, reading in an armchair, in front of a fire. Hope enters. The man jumps up and grabs his cane.

Man What the Devil? Who are you?

Hope I'm Hope, sir.

Man What are you doing in my house? How did you get here?

Hope Through the sewers, with a man who wanted to rob you. But I left him down there 'cos I never wanted to rob no one. I want your help, sir.

Man I think a constable might provide the best assistance here.

Hope No, sir – please. No constab . . .

She breaks off, staring at his chair. Music – 'inside outside' theme.

Man What is it?

Hope That's Jasmine Trellis. The design, I mean. That was his very first one.

Man You know who designed this?

Hope 'Course. William Morris.

Man How can you know that?

Hope I live with him and his wife in Hammersmith.

Man Oh, come now.

Hope It's true. That's why I want your help – to get back to them, safely. Not only Jack o' the Night from the sewers, but constables are looking for me too.

Man What for?

Hope I'm wanted for stealing Jane's jewellery.

Man Jane Morris's jewels? Then a constable is indeed what we need here.

Hope It wasn't me – it was Jack. Would I want to go back if I'd really done it myself? Please – help me.

Man (*ponders*) Very well. I shall come with you to Hammersmith. Let us see if we can find a hansom.

Hope A cab? With horses? I've never been in one of them. (*looking round*) Where's everyone?

Man Everyone?

Hope Your wife and children – are they asleep?

Man I have no wife or children.

Hope Ain't you lonely?

Man Sometimes.

Hope That's sad.

Man Some things in this world *are* sad. Our expectations are not always fulfilled. Now – before we depart, let us check the sewer grill to see if this ruffian is still there. If not, where is his home?

Hope Clerkenwell, sir.

Man Then we shall go to Hammersmith via Clerkenwell. Do not be afraid – I shall be with you.

> *Music – 'thread' theme – as they leave. The scene changes to Clerkenwell Green. They re-enter.*

Still no sign.

Hope We could ask in the coffee house. If Jack's about, they'll have wind of it.

A scruffy woman enters as they turn.

Sir – the hat she's wearing.

Man What of it?

Hope It's Jack's – I'm sure.

Man (*to woman*) One moment please! That hat – how did you come by it?

Scruffy Woman I found it. I was at Blackfriars – down by the river. And I saw it caught on the grills of the Fleet outlet – you know, where it flows into the Thames.

Man Is that all you saw there?

Scruffy Woman Yes, sir – nothing else. Why d'you ask?

Man No matter. That is all. Thank you.

The scruffy woman leaves.

He must have been drowned by the tide. I doubt the body will ever be found.

Hope I killed him.

Man No. He forced you down there. He knew the risks. You must attach no blame to yourself. Now – to Hammersmith.

A beggar-girl enters with white stick and a bowl. She wears a scarf.

Beggar Penny for the blind. Spare a penny for the blind.

Man My dear . . . (*He drops a coin into the bowl.*)

Beggar Thank you, sir. (*Feels the coin.*) But sir – you've made a mistake. This is no penny – but a sovereign.

Man No mistake, my dear. (*to Hope*) Now – let us get on.

Hope I know that voice. (*Pause.*) Stella?

Stella (*it is indeed she*) Hope? Is that Hope?

Hope It can't be. Is this really you, Stella?

Stella removes the scarf.

Stella Yes, Hope – it's me.

Hope But . . . blind? What have they done to you?

Stella They put me on the streets. My eyes had got very bad. Living out they got worse and . . . well – you can see.

Hope Oh, Stella. Stella – it's too cruel.

Stella Life is horrible, Hope. Sometimes I wish I was dead.

Hope No. No – you mustn't say that. We're together again. We can change things. I can make a new life for you.

Stella How?

Hope I've got some new friends, with a lovely house. I'm sure they'll welcome you. (*to man*) Can we take Stella with us?

Man Of course. You can tell me the whole story as we go.

They leave. Scene changes to Hammersmith. Morris works aggressively on a wood block. Jane enters.

Jane William – what *are* you doing?

Morris I am making a new wood block. What does it look like?

Jane But why so furiously?

Morris Because I *am* furious. I trusted her.

Jane You shouldn't expect change overnight, Utopia tomorrow. Life isn't that simple.

Morris slams the wood block down in frustration.

No doubt you're also angry because you have not proved Mr Wardle wrong.

Morris Mr Wardle is but a small matter. What is important is whether or not we can change humanity. Whether a criminal is made instead of simply being born – and therefore can be un-made. Whether a thief need remain a thief forever!

Jane William, calm down. You'll make yourself ill.

Morris I do not care.

Jane Well, you should. You cannot help humanity if you are sick.

Morris is now examining some printed fabric.

Morris Oh, blast!

Jane What now?

Morris I have been trying a new mixture for bleaching out parts of the indigo. But it still is not working.

Jane Then you must try again. Let us hope you succeed before you explode.

Morris Let us hope? I hope the word Hope is never heard in this house again!

Hope enters.

Hope You can't mean that. (*Pause.*) I didn't take that jewellery.

Morris No? Then who did?

Hope Jack o' the Night.

Morris And where might he be?

Hope In the sewers. Dead.

Morris How convenient. The jewellery with him no doubt.

Hope That's right.

Morris No, Hope – that is *not* right. I do not believe a word you say.

Jane Nor I. There is too much evidence against you.

The old man and Stella enter.

Man But there is also much evidence *for* her. She came to my house, having just escaped from this villain, Jack – who is indeed dead in the sewers, there is evidence of that. She could have run off. But no, she wanted me to help her back here. That is hardly the action of a guilty party.

Morris You would make a good lawyer, sir. But who are you? And who (*indicating Stella*) is this?

Before the man can reply Hope butts in very fast:

Hope He lives alone in a big house above the sewers with the wild boar and he's got a chair with Jasmine Trellis on it and we saw this scruffy woman in Clerkenwell with Jack's hat so we know he's dead and this is my friend Stella and she's lost her sight 'cos they put her out on the streets and . . . and . . . and I haven't been lying to you! I haven't! I haven't!

Pause. Suddenly Morris hugs Hope.

Morris I was wrong. Forgive me for not believing you. (*brightening*) Then a thief can become honest. Humanity can change!

Jane (*to Stella*) My dear . . . er . . .

Hope Stella.

Jane Stella – you are shivering.

Stella I've been very poorly, ma'am.

Jane Come through to the kitchen. I'll make some hot milk. Hope – would you fetch a blanket.

Hope darts off as Jane leads Stella out.

Man You are pleased to see her then.

Morris Yes, of course.

Man For herself – not just for your ideals?

Morris For both.

Man Well, it is a pleasure to meet you, Mr Morris. I admire your work greatly. I have also heard some of your views on social change – which make me wonder why you are not actively engaged in politics.

Morris I support the most progressive elements in our parliament, sir.

Man But what are they doing to prevent things like having that poor, blind girl begging on our streets? I would love to see some of your energy more directly involved in changing our society.

Morris Well, sir – perhaps you will. Now – might I offer you a drink?

He leads the old man off. Music. Lights up on Hope, creeping forward, watching something intently. She settles down with pad and pencil and draws. Morris enters behind her. Hope sighs in annoyance as her eyes follow something up into the air. She draws again, then becomes aware of Morris.

Hope I didn't know you were there.

Morris I did not mean to startle you. You have been drawing?

Hope Yeah.

Morris May I see?

Hope It's not very good. Just a picture of a thief who'll always be a thief – who just stole something from you.

Morris What? (*Looks at her pad.*) A bird?

Hope It was stealing your strawberries. And always will given the chance. It won't change.

Morris No – nor it will.

Hope Just as long as he leaves some for us, eh?

   Morris is in a reverie. Music – 'inside outside' theme.

Morris This could make a wonderful design. The bird – in beige and browns.

Hope The foliage in different shades of green.

Morris The flowers . . .?

Hope Pink and white.

Morris The strawberries . . .?

Hope Splashes of bright red.

Morris And all against a blue background. The Strawberry Thief.

   The music ends.

If only I could perfect the indigo dyeing. Then all those colours would be possible – together in one fabulous design.

Hope Why's it so difficult?

Morris The process is complicated. First I dye plain cloth in the indigo vat.

Hope So it comes out blue.

Morris Then I take a wood block with bleaching agents on it and press it onto the cloth. That removes the blue completely from some areas – and lightens it in others. Then I half-dry the cloth, warm it, and then use another wood block to fix an agent in the areas where I want my next colour – yellow.

Hope So it goes in the weld vat.

Morris Yes. Then I carefully repeat the whole process before I plunge it in the next vat for the red sections.

Hope With madder, madder, madder!

Morris That's right. But despite my care measuring the ingredients, it always goes wrong.

Hope Could it be something to do with the cloth then?

Morris No – absolutely not.

Hope What about the temperature you warm it to?

Morris Accurate to a degree.

Hope Then I wonder if it's the water. Won't that be a bit different in every river?

Morris Well, yes – yes it would be.

Hope You need the perfect river then.

Morris (*nods*) Perhaps that should be my main aim in securing new workshops. I am seeing some more premises this afternoon. The water may make the decision for me.

Stella enters but remains separate from them.

Hope All these beautiful colours we work with. I wish Stella could see them.

Morris Yes. She's full of questions about it all.

Hope It's so cruel she can see nothing.

The following song should build a sense of excitement similar to 'inside outside', creating Morris's design world. Here coloured light pierces the darkness to mirror what Stella 'sees'.

Song – Blind World (Stella).

Stella
Such a dark world – A stark and dark world
No spark is hurled inside my eyes
My black and white world – Is now a night world
No stitches purled, no bright surprise

Yet I am not blind – That's what I'm not, blind
I've got my mind to investigate
I see through this blind – Give it a miss, blind
I'm not resigned to a misty fate

I can touch red – So much to touch, red
Such roots I spread, then hold them fast
I can smell blue – That's how I tell blue
That's how I view the spell it's cast

It's clear to me that I can see
More than they know
It's clear to me how I can see
The touch, the smell, the taste
And very sound – of indigo

Hope goes to Stella.

Hope Can you really work out the colours?

Stella Yes. I can see them – in my own way.

Hope Then we can work on the dyes together.

Stella Yes. Oh, how I like it here. Such kind people.

Hope Yeah. They'd probably take us to Ascot if we asked.

Stella To Ascot?

Hope You ain't forgotten?

Stella 'Course not.

Hope We'd have to dress up.

Stella Posh? Like you did all that time ago?

Hope Yeah – like Lady Whatsit. Except I don't really want to be like that. We don't need her. Or Ascot. Not when we've got all this.

Stella No. This is all we need. Hullo, Mr Morris.

Hope turns in surprise. Then Morris enters.

Morris How did you know it was not someone else coming?

Stella Everyone's footsteps are different. I can smell you too.

Morris You mean I need a bath?

Stella No. It's just your personal smell. It's not nasty.

Morris Well, I am pleased to hear it. But you look tired, Stella.

Stella I am a bit.

Morris Hope, I have told you before not to wear her out. She is very frail.

Stella Please – it's not Hope's fault. I'll rest now.

Morris Good. Now, I have some news. I have found the most wonderful new premises at Merton Abbey Mills.

Scene changes to Merton during the following speech, with music – 'thread' theme.

It has everything. Light, airy, workshops with the inspiration of the countryside all around. Ample space for dyeing and drying. Above all, Hope – there is the River Wandle with the purest, softest water imaginable. If I cannot perfect the indigo process here, then I swear it cannot be done anywhere.

He leaves. Hope and Stella now at Merton.

Hope He was right. It's beautiful.

Stella The air's so fresh. And I can hear the river.

Hope There's fish – and ducks.

Stella (*sniffs*) And lots of flowers. No wonder he likes it here.

Morris enters carrying a wood block.

Morris Indeed – is it not perfect? But the best thing is that the indigo process is working at last. You were right, Hope – the water was the key. We are about to print the next pattern – here at Indigo Mill. I know you will love this. (*Pause.*) Hope?

Hope (*distracted*) Sorry? What was that?

Morris This is the wood block for my latest pattern. Hope – what is it?

Hope (*still distracted*) I don't know. It's . . . Can I explore a bit?

Morris Of course. Then join me at the workshops.

Stella Can I come with you, Mr Morris?

Morris Forgive me. In my excitement I have not been paying you proper attention. You look exhausted. Take my arm.

As he leads her off, she almost falls. Morris helps her. Her hand presses against the wood block.

Stella Is that the pattern – Strawberry Thief? For Hope? How clever.

Morris Come inside. You really must rest.

Hope is left alone.

Hope What is it? What is it about this place? There is something . . .

She breaks off as the low mysterious music begins.

The memory – is that from here?

Blue light, rippling.

Is the pattern the water – the river? Yes – yes, this is the place.

Circular movement (the Merton mill-wheel).

Of course! Turning in the mist – the mill-wheel. I've been here before. Where's my shadowy figure?

A figure appears in the mist. A voice echoes 'more'.

Hope This is the thread I've wanted to find for so long. Please – tell me what 'more' means.

Voice 'More' is what Hope must demand.

The figure starts to leave.

Hope Wait! I know who you are! Father!

Abrupt lighting change. All the magic disappears.

Father?

Joe (*stepping forward*) Me – your father? I hardly think so.

Hope Didn't you just say that 'more' is what I must demand?

Joe (*frowns*) I never said a word.

Hope looks past him.

No one down there. That just leads to my farm.

Hope I know it was him. He was here.

Joe I think you've been imagining things. It must be the light or something – because looking at you, I could almost imagine . . . but that's not possible.

Hope It's more than just imagining. Does someone repeating the word 'more' over and over mean anything to you?

Joe Well, yes – yes, it does. Then it's not a trick of the light. I do recognise you. You're Hope.

Hope How do you know my name?

Joe You look just like your father. I knew your parents. They were my neighbours here, years ago. I knew you when you were no bigger than this. Before that dreadful day – when you were taken.

Hope Taken?

Joe Stolen. Lots of children were – to work in factories or wherever. We knew you'd been taken – but we never found out where to.

Hope Then my parents never dumped me on the street, like Stitchit said.

Joe Dump you? Lord, no. They searched for you for years.

Hope Where are they now?

Joe I'm sorry – but they're both dead.

Hope Dead. (*Pause.*) What were they like?

Joe They were good people. She was so strong and kind. And he fought against injustice all his life. He suffered it as a child himself – so he wanted to do all he could to stop it happening to others. He wanted more for them, too.

Hope Then he did say 'more'.

Joe (*nods*) He used to whisper it in your ear as you lay in your cot as a baby. More food for the starving. More homes for the homeless. More care for the sick. More justice for the persecuted. He wanted you to stand firm, head held high, asking for more.

Hope Then I will. They loved me. They never dumped me. And they lived here. It wasn't a dream. It was a real memory. I've found the thread.

Joe leaves as music begins.

Song – The Thread of Life (Hope).

How I know – How now I know
Here's the thread of my life
I've unravelled the mystery
Travelling back through my history
Down the line
Now I've picked up the thread
How I've picked up my life
Now I've picked up the stitch in time
From the thread of my life – Hope

Stella! Stella!

She rushes to find Stella, seated with the wood block on her lap.

Stella – I've got such news, you'll never believe.

She shakes her, thinking she's asleep. Stella slumps forward.

Hope Stella? Stella! No!

Morris and Jane rush in. He feels Stella's pulse.

Morris I'm sorry, Hope. I knew she was terribly weak. I had already sent for the doctor.

Hope It's not fair. (*Pause.*) It's not fair!

Hope goes completely wild, knocking the wood block to the floor, then grabbing some of Morris's designs and ripping them to shreds. Morris gently stops her.

Morris No, Hope – no. That will not help. It cannot help Stella. It will not help you either.

Hope But it's not fair. Why should good people die? After all she's suffered, it's not fair.

Morris No. But this world is not a fair place. It is cruel and unjust. But despair will not help. We must work for change. That is the best way for us to remember Stella. We must try and stop others suffering as she did.

Hope I know – we must work for more. But it's so difficult.

Morris hugs her. Jane picks up the wood block.

Jane Did you see what it is, Hope? William made it especially for you. It's called Strawberry Thief.

Hope Strawberry Thief?

Morris Yes. Will we print it, Hope?

Hope For Stella. Yes – yes, of course we will.

During the final song, the stage is cleared and Strawberry Thief is produced, the stage becoming full of swathes of the repeated image – a space alive with colour and design . . . and hope.

Song – The Thread of Life (all).

Here is my home – Indigo Mill
The water so bright – The wheel turning still

Morris

Strawberry Thief – Printed and dyed
Like Hope it appears – And won't be denied

Morris/Hope/Jane

Lives can be changed – Nothing is still
With courage and hope we must have the will
For more – more – more – more – more

Hope

How I know – How I now know
Here's the thread of my life
I've unravelled the mystery
Travelling back through my history
Down the line
Now I've picked up the thread
How I've picked up my life
Now I've picked up the stitch in time
From the thread of my life – Hope

All

More – more – more – more – more

Good luck Hope – Don't give up Hope
With the thread of your life
You've unravelled the mystery
Travelling back through your history
Down the line
You have picked up the thread
You have picked up your life
You have picked up the stitch in time
From the thread of your life – Hope
Hope goes on
Hope goes on

BODY TALK

Andy Rashleigh

Characters

with doubling for seven actors

Inside Mudge	*Inside Tidge*
Braino	
Moutho	**Tummia**
Tummo	**Ms Memory**
Artlungs	**Brainia**
Mr Memory/ White Corpuscle 1	**Mouthia**
Bottom Ender/ White Corpuscle 2	
Germ	

*The set represents the control room inside the head
of a child. It is situated somewhere in the sinuses
behind the eyes.*

*The control room is peopled by Bods – Brain, Mouth,
Tum, etc. They are heads of the departments that run the
daily life of the child. At times we are in a boy called
Mudge's head and at others we are in a girl called Tidge's
head. The difference should be clear from the respective
Bods' behaviour and the changeover should not be
cumbersome: most probably done with lighting.*

*On the stage and in the audience are television screens,
which show the view through each child's eyes. This is*

pre-recorded video. The screens are not always switched on because each Brain has its own private screen, and anyway most everyday things the children do are done on automatic pilot.

Brain's brainbox is the flight-deck that controls the body movements and thoughts of the child.

Mouth has a microphone into which he/she speaks as the child's voice.

In Mudge's head Artlungs sits at a machine which he/she pumps all the time. The machine could be like a harmonium crossed with a rowing machine. In Tidge's head the machine is automatic.

Mr/Ms Memory have memory banks offstage. The Tums have access to the Nether Regions.

Author's Note

If anyone performs this play they'll need a pre-recorded video of what happens in the outside world. It's possible, as in the first production at The Unicorn, that the edited video will not quite match the dialogue in the script. Please feel free to tinker with my dialogue to make it fit, rather than fret about loyalty to the text. Remember it's a play and, as Artlungs might say, 'If it doesn't work on the stage, there's not much point to it then.'

Act One

At the beginning of the play we are in Mudge's head. It is night. He is going to bed.

Voice Over
> Behind the eyes of every boy, between the ears
>   in every girl,
> Under your brows, above your nose, is where
>   you'll find another world.
> A world of Bods who run your life; who fly you,
>   as you'd fly a plane,
> From when you're born to when you die, and
>   Captain of them all is Brain.

> *Lights up on Braino at his control desk.*
>   *Screen – Mudge's point of view. View down the bed*
> *from the pillow.*

Braino Prepare Our Boy for sleep mode. The Mum is on her way upstairs. Ready for goodnight kiss and lights out.

Voice Over
> For Brain is wise and Brain is clever: does what's
>   best without a doubt,
> He's good as gold and he would never stir up
>   trouble, unlike Mouth!

> *Screen – Mudge's point of view. The Mum comes into*
> *the bedroom.*

Braino Mouth! Organise your department for a goodnight kiss with The Mum.

Moutho I'm busy.

Moutho and Tummo are playing draughts on the floor with gigantic 'Smarties'.

Braino Now, Mouth!

Moutho (*to Tummo*) No cheating while I'm away.

Screen – Mudge's point of view. The Mum tucks Mudge up.

The Mum Night, night, sleep tight, don't let the bugs bite.

Moutho (*into microphone*) Night night, Mum.

Screen – Mudge's point of view. The Mum kisses him, turns off the light and goes out.

(*returning to Tummo*) She always says that. Tch!

Braino Brainbox off duty for the night. Screen off. Automatic pilot. Sleep mode on. Alarm set for 07.00 hours.

Braino switches off lots of knobs on his console. The screen goes blank. Braino walks down with a clipboard to where Tummo and Moutho are playing draughts.

Department reports for the day. Mouth, how are things with you?

Moutho Teeth in good shape. Spit flowing well.

Braino 'Saliva' if you don't mind.

Moutho Tongue a bit furry this morning but says he feels fine now.

Braino Good.

Moutho Request from Canine Teeth for no more celery. It gets between them and the Incisors.

Braino Request noted and refused. Celery's good for Our Boy. By the way, what on earth are you two up to?

Voice Over
It's not just Mouth who wastes his time, there's
his great chum
His pal and buddy, bestest friend – Mouth's
playmate, Tum.

Braino I said what are you doing?

Tummo What does it look like?

Braino Don't you be surly with me, Tummy.

Tummo My name is not 'Tummy'. It is Tum. I mean, do we call you 'Brainy'?

Moutho We certainly do not.

Braino (*picking up a Smarty*) What are these?

Moutho Smarties. And leave that alone. I was just going to do this.

Moutho jumps two, takes them off the board and throws them into the exit to the mouth.

You're in trouble now, Tum.

Tummo No, I'm not.

Tummo jumps the rest of Moutho's Smarties with his remaining Smarty and wins.

Braino How come we've got Smarties?

Moutho We bought them at the corner shop on the way home from school.

Braino No we didn't.

Tummo Mouth asked for them when you were thinking

about buying that geography magazine.

Braino So that's why we couldn't afford it.

Tummo takes the remaining Smarties to the mouth exit and throws them down.

Tummo Mind your heads, Teeth. More on the way.

Braino You can't let the Teeth chew those.

Moutho Why not? It's what Teeth are for.

Braino Not now. Our Boy's in bed. We already brushed them.

Tummo Well, it's better than sending them straight down to my department unchewed.

Braino This is just not good enough. This calls for a serious word with all department heads first thing tomorrow. In the meantime, Tum, your report please.

Tummo Gastric Juices want more food.

Braino They always want more food.

Tummo That's all.

Braino What about the Bottom End?

Tummo The Bottom Enders always want less food. Except celery and prunes. They seem to like them. Can't think why.

Braino Always plenty of those if only Mouth would ask for them once in a while.

Moutho Yuk.

Braino Right now. Get some sleep, we've got an important day ahead of us tomorrow.

Braino goes to Mr Memory as Tummo and Moutho settle down to sleep.

Voice Over
They need their sleep, for tomorrow at school
There is a test in Geography.
Responsible for doing well is Mr Memory.

Braino Well, Mr Memory! Your department report for the day.

Mr Memory Fine. Everything's fine.

Braino Ready for the big day?

Mr Memory Yes. Yes. Very ready. Night, night.

Braino (*disbelieving*) Yes. Goodnight. Lights down.

Braino punches the department reports into his brainbox and settles down to sleep.

Moutho (*loud whisper*) Mr Memory. Mr Memory.

Mr Memory What do you want, Mouth?

Moutho A story.

Tummo Yeah. Tell a story.

Mr Memory Not tonight.

Tummo Why not.

Mr Memory I . . . I don't feel like it tonight.

Braino Is that talking, I hear? Not telling one of your silly stories, Mr Memory.

Mr Memory No, Brain.

Braino I should hope not. Sooner you clear them out of the Memory Banks and get some good solid facts in the better.

Moutho (*whisper*) But you always tell us one.

Tummo We like them. We want a story.

Tummo and Moutho Story, story, story, story, story.

Mr Memory All right. Which one? no no not tonight

Tummo The one about the boy. In the village.

Mr Memory Which boy?

Tummo The one that sang.

Mr Memory Oh, yes.

Tummo I love it. It makes me cry.

Mr Memory I can't remember how it starts.

Tummo As far away as a map could say . . .

Mr Memory Oh yes . . . As far away as a map could say, to the right of . . .

Moutho A town called Wrong.

Mr Memory Town called Wrong . . .

Moutho In a village as old –

Mr Memory Village as old.

Moutho and Tummo As the snow is cold, was a boy who sang –

Mr Memory A song.

Tummo A haunting song.

Mr Memory You seem to know it. Tell it to each other.

Moutho No.

Mr Memory Not tonight. See you in the morning.

Tummo Spoilsport.

Mr Memory Leave me alone. Don't you two start getting at me as well.

Voice Over
  He couldn't remember the tales he knew,
  Mr Memory wasn't the same.
  He'd forgotten the lot, no idea what to do,
  Just couldn't live up to his name.

Moutho Goodnight, Tum.

Tummo Goodnight, Mouth.

Moutho Goodnight, Mr Memory.

Mr Memory Goodnight, Mouth. Goodnight, Tum.

Tummo Goodnight, Mr Memory.

Moutho Sleep well, Tum.

Tummo Sleep well, Mouth.

Moutho Sleep well, Mr Memory.

Braino For crying out loud, will you lot shut up!

Moutho Goodnight, Brain.

Tummo Goodnight, Brain.

Braino Aaargh!

Voice Over
  So through the night the Bods can rest
  And wake their boy up keen and bright.
  But there is one who gets no sleep;
  It's Heart and Lungs whose job's to keep
  The pumps all working through the night.

Artlungs Brain.

Braino What is it Artlungs?

Artlungs We are friends, aren't we.

Braino Yes, Art.

Artlungs And you know what you promised.

Braino Yes, Art.

Artlungs Say it again. Go on.

Braino If Mr Memory messes up the test then I'll let you take over the Memory Banks.

Artlungs Thank you. You're my best friend.

Braino For a trial period.

Artlungs Nighty night, Brain. Sleep well.

Braino And you. I mean . . . Have a good night, yourself.

Artlungs 'Have a good night'! All right for you lot. I never get any sleep. Yet. I just go on and on. Pump, pump, pump. The mouth of a river's called an estuary. Pump, pump, pump. Terminal moraine. Pump, pump, pump. Artesian wells in the Nile Valley. Pump, pump, pump, rumpy dumpy pumpy pump.

Tummo Put a sock in it, Art!

Artlungs Drumlins! Pump, pump, pump, pump.

Voice Over
    The night has passed, the early birds go catching
        worms and milkmen call,
    The papers come, it's break of day.
    The Mum and Dad begin to stir, as do the Bods,
        well rested all;
    Though Heart and Lungs still pumps away.

Lights up. Braino, Moutho, Tummo and Mr Memory are all still asleep.

Artlungs Must be morning by now. I said, *'It Must Be Morning By Now'*.

Tummo (*stirring*) It's not time to get up yet.

Artlungs Get up. *Get Up!* Chance'd be a fine thing.

Tummo (*trying to get back to sleep*) Shut up, Art.

Artlungs I am not an Art. I am a Heart. With a 'haitch'. Heart and Lungs, two jobs in one, no breaks, no holidays, no fun.

Tummo Whoever you are, belt up.

Artlungs Wonder what it's like to be asleep? Nice I'd think by the look of that lot. Elevating. Good word. Put that in my memory bank. L.E.V . . . Mr Memory, how do you spell 'elevating'? Mr Memory!

Mr Memory (*stirring*) No idea.

Artlungs Knew you wouldn't have. Pump, pump, pump. All day, all night, all day, all night, all day again, all night again, while you lot get eight hours off every night. Don't you, Mouth? Hey! (*no reply*) Huh. Hey, Tum! Are you still awake? Tum. Tum, Tum, Tummy. Gut. Stomach. Abdomen. Belly. Belly, Belly, Belly, Belly, Belly, Belly, Belly –

Tummo leaps up and goes over to Artlungs. He pushes his finger in his face.

Tummo My name is Tum! Got it.

Artlungs Okay.

Tummo T.O.M. Right!

Artlungs 'U'.

Tummo Me.

Artlungs T.U.M.

Tummo What?

Artlungs That's how you spell 'Tum'. Ha! Can't even spell your own name.

Tummo (*very angry*) Shut it!

Artlungs Fine.

Tummo Good.

Artlungs If you say so.

Tummo I do.

Tummo slopes off back to his sleeping area.

T.U.M.?

Artlungs Aha.

Tummo Don't believe you.

Artlungs True.

Tummo I'll check with Mr Memory when he wakes up and if you're lying –

Artlungs He won't know. He knows nothing. You get to be good at spelling when you don't have any sleep. Ever.

Tummo (*settling down to sleep*) Don't start all that again.

Artlungs I'll tell you what I am. B.O.R.D. What does that spell?

Tummo (*going to sleep*) Don't care.

Artlungs You don't care. Mr Memory doesn't care. Mouth says he cares but he'll say anything. Brain cares. Brain's my friend. Aren't you, Brain?

Artlungs gets up from his machine. He walks over to Braino and gradually as though his battery is going

*down goes into slow motion. The lights fade. An alarm
goes off. 'Heart malfunction' is heard over the sound
system. Other Bods wake up and in slow motion
Braino and Tummo thrust Artlungs back onto his
machine.*

Braino (*slow and deep*) What on earth do you think
you're doing, you idiot?

*They get Artlungs pumping away again and Braino
gets his normal voice back.*

Have you gone mad?

Tummo He nearly killed us all.

Mr Memory He what?

Artlungs I'm fed up.

Moutho wakes up.

Moutho What happened?

Artlungs I wanted a rest. Everybody gets some sleep but
me.

Tummo Glue him to the seat.

Artlungs You're always getting at me.

Moutho Are you surprised? Every day it's moan, moan,
moan.

Artlungs You'd moan if you did this all day.

Moutho How much longer have we got to live, Mr
Memory?

Mr Memory No idea.

Moutho Brain?

Braino How should I know?

Moutho How long do people live? Someone must know.

Tummo Don't look at me.

Mr Memory Our Boy's Great Grandma's a hundred and eighty-four. I think.

Moutho One hundred and eighty-four! So if we live that long we've got a hundred and . . . loads more years of listening to this fool moaning on.

Artlungs Don't have to.

Braino How do you mean?

Artlungs I just get off this and we stop breathing and –

He gets off. Lights fade: alarm bells ring. The others rush to put him back.

At least it makes you notice me. Even when I shouted 'Fire' yesterday nobody so much as turned a hair.

Braino We're in the middle of an eleven-year-old boy's head. Where's the fire going to come from?

Artlungs Sorry, Brain. Friend. I'll not move till you tell me I can have his job.

Braino Shush. I'm busy.

Tummo Like I said. Glue him to it.

Braino Hey! My records show we failed to wash our boy's feet last night.

Artlungs Yuk. Smelleee.

Moutho Who's fault is that then?

Braino Not my job.

Moutho So whose job is it?

Braino The hands. The hands have to wash the feet.

Moutho And who controls the hands? You do, Brain!

Braino And who's supposed to ask if we can have a bath? You are, Mouth. Like you asked for Smarties when I wasn't paying attention.

Moutho Mr Memory, when did we last have a bath?

Mr Memory Not my job. I'm only 'what we learn'. It's Brain who's supposed to remember 'what we do'.

Tummo So it is your fault.

Braino I . . . We were going to have a bath last night but you ate too much, Tum. So Our Boy's Mum said we couldn't in case we got cramp.

Moutho What is he burbling on about?

Braino And while I was busy talking to Mr Memory about today's test, you and Tum plotted to ask for seconds of apple crumble. And I heard you say, 'Please Mummy, could I have a leeettle bit more, please?'

Moutho I don't talk like that.

Braino And then we finished off the custard, so we couldn't have a bath; and then there were the Smarties. So that's that. I've decided. I'm Brain. I'm in charge. There's going to be some discipline in this body from now on. We must not be late today, so I'll stir Our Boy and see what the time is.

  He goes over to his private monitor.

Tummo It's not nearly time to get up.

Moutho I think we'd all like to see what the time is.

Tummo Not that we don't trust you or anything.

Braino Harrumph. If you insist. Eyes opening now.

Main screen on.

> *Screen – Mudge's point of view. Alarm clock by the side of the bed that says it is 6.55.*

Moutho Hang on. It's only five to seven. Everybod back to bed for five minutes.

Braino So that we are well prepared today, we will get Our Boy up five minutes early and get ready for school now. Isn't that a good idea, Mr Memory?

Mr Memory Er, ye-e-es.

Braino Good then, chop chop. But, to conserve our energies for the test, as a special treat, all getting out of bed, dressing, washing, breakfasting and going to school will be done on automatic pilot!

> *This doesn't get the ovation he expected.*

Come on, you all love it when we go on automatic pilot.

Artlungs Except me. No Automatic Pilot for me, is there?

Braino So we'll go on automatic pilot and you can sit about, play cards, go for a walk down the right nostril, make wax models in the ear, do what you like as long as there are no emergencies.

Tummo Can we play trampoline on the waggler?

Braino The what?

Tummo The . . . what's it called, Mr Memory?

Mr Memory I can't remember.

Artlungs I think he means the uvula.

Tummo That's it. The waggly thing at the top of the throat.

Moutho No.

Tummo You used to let us bounce around on that.

Moutho That's before we could speak. What happens if I have to say anything? You'll get pinged off and fly through the lips and . . . and . . .

Braino And then we wouldn't have a Tum.

Artlungs Good thing too. If we didn't have a Tum, Our Boy'd get much thinner and I wouldn't have to work so hard.

Tummo (*going for him*) And where do you think you get the energy to pump, pump, pump in the first place.

Artlungs Not from seconds of apple crumble.

Tummo (*pushing him*) Yes you do. Ask Mr Memory.

Artlungs (*pushing back*) Ask him yourself.

Tummo Don't you push me.

> *Artlungs gets off, they start fighting and everything goes into slow motion. Braino and Moutho put Artlungs back and lead Tummo away.*

Braino Right, no automatic pilot. Hands on, full activity. If you can't be trusted to amuse yourselves in your free time then better you're kept busy.

Artlungs Hee, hee.

Braino I'll just take a few moments to decide what we are going to wear today.

Moutho We always wear what Our Boy's Mum puts out.

Braino Yes, but I have to work out which order to put it on in.

Tummo No wonder we're stupid if that's our Brain.

Moutho You all right, Mr M?

Mr Memory Er . . .

Tummo What's up? Bad dreams.

Moutho Tell us one of your dreams, go on.

Mr Memory (*whisper*) Look, don't tell those two, but . . . this geography test today.

Moutho What about it?

Mr Memory I can't remember a thing.

Moutho What?

Mr Memory I couldn't even remember the story last night, could I?

Moutho That's true.

Mr Memory Ask me a question.

Tummo How do you spell 'Tum'?

Mr Memory Come on, it's T.U.M, even you know that. I heard Brain and Artlungs talking. Artlungs wants a change and Brain said he'd think about it.

Moutho A change!

Mr Memory To my job. While we're asleep at night he learns new things. Ask him some geography.

Tummo Artlungs.

Artlungs Not talking to you.

Tummo What's . . .?

Mr Memory Ask him the capital of France.

Moutho Art, what's the capital of France.

Artlungs Paris, of course.

Moutho Is that right?

Mr Memory I think it might be. But I'm not sure. See!

Tummo But if he became Mr Memory he'd be down here with us all day and you'd be stuck over there.

Mr Memory No sleep. Ever. Pump, pump, pump.

Moutho And we'd have to play with him.

Artlungs Want to know the capital of Italy?

Moutho No thanks.

Artlungs It's Rome.

Tummo Is it?

Mr Memory Don't ask me.

Artlungs Want to know what a hanging valley is?

Tummo What shall we do, Mouth?

Artlungs An ox-bow lake?

Moutho Smarty Plan A.

Mr Memory What's that?

Moutho Get down those tubes, Tum, and have a word with your lads –

Tummo About the Smarties?

Moutho Yes. Spread the story that there's a chance of a day in bed if they can bluff Brain that there was a germ in the Smarties and we've got Stomach Ache so bad that we can't –

Tummo Great. I'll bring one of the Bottom Enders up here to confirm it, shall I?

Mr Memory (*wrinkling his nose*) Pooh, that's going a bit far.

Moutho (*to Tummo*) No, it's good thinking, Tum.

A loud voice booms over the intercom.

The Mum Mudge! Mudge! Wake up will you, you're late.

Tummo Oh no, it's The Mum.

The Bods rock about as Mudge is shaken.

Moutho Why does she always have to shake us about?

Braino Stabilisers go! Action stations! Screen on!

Screen – Mudge's point of view. The Mum staring straight into his eyes.

The Mum Mustn't be late or you'll be in trouble with your teacher again.

Moutho Why does she always have to shout first thing in the morning.

Screen – Mudge's point of view. The Mum goes over to curtains and pulls them open.

Braino Volume turned down. Light too bright. Avert eyes.

Screen – Mudge's point of view. Turns to wall.

The Mum Breakfast'll be ready in two minutes.

Screen – Mudge's point of view. Turns to see The Mum leaving. Stares at the ceiling.

Braino You heard her! Come on, *'getting up'* starts now. Where are you going?

Tummo Minor malfunction in the stomach.

He goes down the alimentary canal.

Braino Says nothing here about a malfunction. Getting up now!

Screen – Mudge's point of view. Gets out of bed and goes to the bathroom.

Moutho (*shouting down to Teeth*) Teeth, brace yourselves for morning brush.

Braino I expect you're all rotting after a night covered in chocolate.

Screen – Mudge's point of view. He has reached the bathroom. He looks in the mirror.

Artlungs We're getting spots.

Braino Where?

Artlungs Right cheek.

Braino Focus right cheek.

Screen – Mudge's point of view. Close up of right cheek in the mirror.

Moutho Can't see anything.

Braino Feel it, right hand.

Screen – Mudge's point of view. Right hand comes up to feel the spot.

Yes, there's something there.

Artlungs Yuk, you're not going to squeeze it, are you.

Braino Not big enough yet. Make a note to have salad for school dinner, Tum. Where is Tum?

Moutho He'll be back in sec.

Braino Quick wash and then prepare for evacuation.

Screen – Mudge's point of view. Splashes his face.

Hang on. There's no information from the Bottom End as to whether we need full-scale defecation or just urination this morning.

Artlungs What's he talking about?

Moutho Number ones and number twos.

Artlungs Why can't he say so?

Braino Because Our Boy's Mum wants us to use the proper words and not baby talk. We'll assume it's just Number . . . I mean 'urination'.

Screen – Mudge's point of view. Approaches the toilet and lifts the seat.

Artlungs Do we have to watch?

Moutho Do you good to see how the other half lives.

Braino Close your eyes then.

Artlungs does so. Tummo returns.

Where've you been?

Tummo Bad news, I'm afraid. Scale 1 emergency.

Braino Automatic pilot.

The Screen goes blank.

Tummo (*calls*) Come on up.

A Bottom Ender comes up.

Artlungs Pongee. It's a Bottom Ender.

Braino Don't come any closer. You're not supposed to come up here.

Bottom Ender Why?

Artlungs Stinky poo.

Bottom Ender (*sniffing himself*) I don't stink.

Tummo They're just jealous. I like it.

Bottom Ender Thanks, Tum. Like what?

Tummo Your smell.

Bottom Ender But I don't smell.

Braino What have you brought this Bottom Ender up here for, Tum?

Tummo Terrible news from the Nether Regions, Brain.

Artlungs (*spluttering and flapping more furiously*) I should say.

Moutho Shut up!

Braino Get on with it.

Bottom Ender Well . . . we've got a germ.

Bottom Ender glances at Tummo throughout his badly learnt lie.

Braino What sort of germ?

Bottom Ender A . . . a . . . bottom sort of germ . . .

Tummo nods frantically.

Tummo Must have been in a bit of fluff on a Smarty.

Bottom Ender And it's upsetting us.

Tummo Giving us . . . them . . . a bad attack of the cramps –

Moutho So we'd better go back to bed –

75

Bottom Ender For the rest of the day –

Tummo And rest –

Tummo And read comics –

Moutho (*going to his microphone*) I'll tell The Mum.

Bottom Ender That's that, then. I'll be off. (*to Tummo*) Was I all right?

Braino Stop right there. Mouth! (*goes to his monitor*) Screen on.

Screen – Mudge's point of view. Going downstairs.

Braino We're walking well enough for a boy with the cramps in his bottom end!

Bottom Ender Yes, Brain.

Screen – Mudge's point of view. Goes into the kitchen. The Mum is by the stove. On the table are a packet of Frosties, toast, bacon sandwiches, steaming tea.

Braino Oh, look! Breakfast! Frosties, your favourite, Tum. Bacon sandwich. Toast. Yum, yum.

Tummo is drooling.

Bet it makes you water too, Mouth.

Screen – Mudge's point of view. The Mum turns round.

The Mum You all right this morning, Mudge?

Braino Are we?

The Mum Cat got your tongue? You all right?

Moutho looks at the others and reluctantly says into the microphone.

Moutho (*into microphone*) Yes, I'm fine, Mummy.

The Mum Chop, chop then or you'll be late and your little friend will go without you.

Screen – Mudge's point of view. Mudge pours cereal and milk into his bowl.

Bottom Ender Our little friend?

Tummo That horrible girl next door.

Moutho We have to walk to school with her.

Tummo She's s-o-o-o – pretty –

Moutho And polite –

Tummo And clever –

Moutho We hate her.

Artlungs I like her.

Braino Right, Screen off. Automatic pilot.

The screen goes blank. Braino comes down from his podium.

Now you, get back to the Nether Regions. I don't want to see you again without a very good reason.

Artlungs Or smell you.

Tummo Shut up.

Artlungs 'Scuse me for keeping us alive.

Braino Go!

Bottom Ender Yes. (*to Tummo and Moutho*) Sorry. (*He waddles off down the alimentary canal.*)

Braino I am waiting for an explanation from you two –

He is interrupted by an extraordinarily loud crunching sound.

77

Action stations! What's that? Screen!

Screen – Mudge's point of view. Looking across the kitchen. Everything is normal.

What was that?

Screen – Mudge's point of view. A spoonful of Frosties rise towards the mouth. The crunching noise starts again.

Mouth, is that you making that noise?

Moutho We always make that noise when we eat Frosties. It's just usually I do this. (*He flicks a switch. The crunching stops.*) And turn the volume down.

Braino Screen off!

The screen goes blank.

Moutho Only I didn't feel like it just now!

Braino You are being deliberately obstructive.

Moutho If I knew what that meant I'd probably agree.

Artlungs Obstructive means –

Braino Don't try and come Mr Clever Clogs with me, Mouth. Just remember, the lot of you. I am the Brain. And what do we say? What do we say?

All (*mumbling*) Brain's in charge.

Braino Louder!

All Brain's in charge.

Braino I didn't hear, Mr Memory.

Artlungs He didn't say it.

Braino Mr Memory!

Mr Memory is deep in his files.

Mr Memory. What do we say?

Mr Memory Er. Moscow.

Braino What?

Mr Memory Capital of Spain.

Artlungs No it's not.

Braino What's the Capital of Spain got to do with anything?

Mr Memory I'm revising for the test like you said I should.

Braino What's the Capital of England?

Mr Memory That's too easy.

Braino What's the highest mountain in Scotland?

Mr Memory Everybody knows that.

Braino What's the name of Our Boy's teacher?

Mr Memory Mister –

Braino She's a lady.

Mr Memory Yes. Miss Turner –

Braino She's a Mrs. Come on. I'm waiting for an answer.

Moutho Give him a chance?

Tummo Bully.

Braino I'm waiting.

Mr Memory (bursts into tears) I . . . I can't remember. I . . . I can't remember anything when you bully me.

Tummo (comforting) Mr M.

Moutho Nothing?

Mr Memory No . . .

79

Artlungs That's it then. If he's lost his memory and all he has to do is remember things there's not much point to him is there? I know capital cities and rivers and the name of our teacher. I'll take over and he can –

Braino Wait! So that's what all this germ nonsense was. Protecting Mr Memory! Trying to get off school so Our Boy wouldn't have to take his test.

Tummo Yes, Brain.

Braino If we don't do it today they'll make us do it next week.

Moutho Mr M'll be back to his old self by then. If you two leave him alone.

Braino He'd better be by the time we get to school. Or maybe we could do a swap.

Artlungs Oslo's the Capital of Norway. Warsaw's the Capital of Poland.

Moutho No, Brain, anything but that.

Tummo You don't want him let loose among the rest of us do you?

Artlungs In fourteen hundred and ninety-two Columbus sailed the ocean blue. Richard Of York Gave Battle In Vain. Ten sixty-six, the Battle of Hastings. Twelve fifteen, the Magna Carta.

Braino What else can I do? If Mr Memory doesn't come up with the goods today, they change round tonight.

Tummo No!

Braino Unless you want to let him run the Tummy Department and you take over from Artlungs.

Tummo No.

Braino You sure?

Tummo Yes.

Braino Then let's see you getting on with some work, shall we?

Tummo I . . . I'll get downstairs to make sure we're digesting breakfast properly. (*He slinks off down the alimentary canal.*)

Braino Lost for words, Mouth?

Moutho Er –

Braino Only Artlungs has got a very pleasant speaking voice and if you want a change I'm sure it can be arranged.

Moutho No – I'll just . . . go and have a chatter with the Teeth if it's all right by you.

Braino Fine.

Moutho goes off.

Artlungs Anything else? World records. Tropical birds? Flags of all nations?

Mr Memory Please, Brain. Give me a break.

Braino I might well do that. You might be in line for a very long break indeed!

Lights down.

Voice Over
  Next door to Mudge there lives a girl, she's
    Tidge by name.
  And in her head's another world, not quite the
    same.
  Her Mouth and Tum and Memory all work
    together.

81

Poor Brain's abused, misused and at the end of
her tether.

*Lights up inside Tidge's head. Brainia is at her controls.
Tummia leads Ms Memory and Mouthia in
synchronised aerobics.*

Brainia We are now leaving the house. Remember Our
Girl has to wait for the boy next door.

Mouthia We know, Brain.

Tummia We always have to wait.

Mouthia Because he's always late.

Ms Memory It makes us fulminate.

Tummia We're a poet.

Ms Memory and Mouthia And we don't know it.

Brainia Shall we swing on the gate?

The others look at her in disgust.

Tummia I don't know.

Brainia It was just an idea.

Ms Memory What a notion.

Brainia I thought we might have some fun.

Ms Memory But what would people think?

Tummia Of all things.

Mouthia Must do something about her.

Brainia I'm sorry. Oh. Hang on. The Mummy's waving
goodbye.

Tummia Then put the screen on, slowcoach.

Screen goes on.
  *Screen – Tidge's point of view. The Mummy is
waving from the open front door.*

The Mummy Are you dreaming, dear? I was just saying
bye-bye and good luck.

Mouthia (*into microphone*) Sorry, Mummy. Bye-bye.
Thank you. I can only do my best.

  *Screen – Tidge's point of view. The Mummy blows her
a kiss, goes in and closes the door. Tidge looking about
her, up and down the street.*

Tummia The Mummy might have got cold waiting for us
to notice her.

Ms Memory Why can't you get anything right, Brain?

Brainia Oh dear.

Mouthia Aren't we going to shut the gate after us.

Brainia Yes. Yes, of course.

  Screen – Tidge's point of view. Closing the gate.

Ms Memory It's a good job we're all so smart.

Mouthia And polite.

Tummia And pretty.

All Three That we don't need to use our Brain.

  They titter awfully.
  *Screen – Tidge's point of view. The Postman comes
up to her.*

Mouthia (*into microphone*) Good morning, Mr Postman.

Postman Good morning. What a nice polite little girl you
are.

Mouthia Thank you.

Screen – Tidge's point of view. Postman goes up her path and delivers letters.

Ms Memory I don't like him.

Tummia Nor do I.

Mouthia He's fat.

Ms Memory And old.

Tummia And he smells of smoking a pipe and beer.

All Three Urgh.

Brainia You can't smoke beer.

Screen – Tidge's point of view. The Postman comes back down the path.

Mouthia (*into microphone*) I'm sorry, am I in the way, Mr Postman?

Postman (*smiling*) No, no.

Screen – Tidge's point of view. He goes up the path to next door and as he reaches it, Mudge bursts out and knocks him over. The Mum follows him out.

Watch out, young fellow.

Brainia Here's Mudge.

Tummia We can see.

Screen – Tidge's point of view. The Mum picks up the Postman and his letters.

The Mum Mudge, I've told you to be careful. (*Smiles.*) Hallo there, Tidge. I'm sorry, he's late as usual.

Mouthia (*into microphone*) That's all right, Mrs Mudgington.

Tummia Yuk, look at him.

Ms Memory If I was his Mummy I'd give him a good spanking.

Tummia If I was his Mummy I'd give him a good wash.

Screen – Tidge's point of view. Mudge looks at her and walks on ahead.

Mudge You coming then?

Screen – Tidge's point of view. Following Mudge.

Brainia Walking to school. Automatic pilot. Screen off.

The Screen goes off.

Tummia Do you know what I'd like to do?

Ms Memory What's that?

Tummia Something, something – (*She giggles.*)

Brainia Eat a Mars bar?

Tummia No. (*Covers her ears.*) I can't believe I heard that.

Brainia It would make a change.

Tummia I meant something that might get a certain boy into trouble and keep Our Girl looking good.

Ms Memory I like the sound of this.

Tummia So what about –

She gathers them round her.
Lights down.

Voice Over
So Tidge's Bods now make a plan to cause Mudge
    trouble if they can.
Tidge keeps on walking just behind him,

which is odd –
Or so it seems to Mudge's Bods.

Lights up inside Mudge's head.
    Screen – Mudge's point of view. Walking along the street.

Tummo Why's she walking behind us?

Moutho Don't know.

Tummo She's normally rushing so as to be first at school.

Moutho So she can say –

Tummo and Moutho 'Morning, Sir, I like your tie. Hallo, Miss, what a nice skirt.' Yuk.

Moutho Oi, Brain!

Braino What?

Moutho Check out what's happening behind us.

Braino Why?

Artlungs They want to look at her because she's pretty.

Tummo We do not.

Artlungs I think she's pretty. Wish we were like her.

Moutho We do not.

Braino At least she'll pass the test.

Moutho Go on. Something's up.

Screen – Mudge's point of view. He turns and we see Tidge about to bend down to pick something from the ground. She stops herself when she sees Mudge turn.

(*into microphone*) What are you doing?

Mouthia What's it got to do with you, stupid boy?

Moutho (*into microphone*) Just wondered.

Braino Come on, let's get to school. Get it over with, eh, Mr Memory!

Screen – Mudge's point of view. Carries on walking.

Automatic pilot.

The Screen goes off.

Tummo I tell you, Mouth, she's up to something.

Moutho Keep an eye on that screen of yours, Brain.

Lights down.

Voice Over
Nice Tidge, clever Tidge couldn't be horrid
    whatever they said.
Good girl, pretty girl: not a bad thought in
    the whole of her head.

Lights up inside Tidge's head.
Screen – Tidge's point of view. Following Mudge up the road.

Brainia This is awful. We mustn't do it.

Ms Memory You're the one who wanted to have some fun.

Brainia Not like this. Not at someone else's expense.

Mouthia If we do it properly, no one will know it was us.

Brainia We will. It's deceitful, unfair and wrong. And we . . . I'll feel guilty.

Mouthia Who cares? Everyone'll still think Our Girl's –

Ms Memory Smart –

87

Mouthia And polite –

Tummia (*watching the screen*) There's one.

Mouthia Where?

Tummia Pay attention, Brain. Go back. Look down.

Screen – Tidge's point of view. Looking at a large stone by the roadside.

Pick it up then!

Screen – Tidge's point of view. Picks up the stone and walks on.

Mouthia Great. Now we have to find a suitable –

Screen – Tidge's point of view. Mudge turns round suspiciously.

Tummia Hide it.

Mouthia (*into microphone*) What are you looking at?

Screen – Tidge's point of view. Mudge walks on.

There. Look over there.

Screen – Tidge's point of view. Passing a garden in which there is a greenhouse.

Brainia No. We mustn't.

Tummia This'll really get him into trouble.

Brainia I refuse.

Ms Memory Then we'll have to take over.

Tummia Will you be able to manage?

Ms Memory I think so.

Brainia I'm not going to do it.

Tummia You don't have to.

Tummia and Ms Memory bundle Brainia off her podium. Tummia holds her down as Ms Memory takes over the controls.

Mouthia Can you remember how to use the arms?

Brainia Get off me.

Ms Memory Yes. Here goes.

Brainia It's mutiny.

Ms Memory Only need the right arm. This one here.

The Screen goes blank.

Mouthia You've switched the screen off.

Ms Memory This one then.

The volume of traffic and bird song gets very loud.

No. Yes. Found it. Here we go.

Lights down.

Voice Over
With the stone in her hand and her arm in the air,
And Tidge wound up to let it go,
Mudge wondering what she's up to, turns
And sees that she's about to throw.

Lights up inside Mudge's head.
Screen – Mudge's point of view. Tidge throws the stone at the greenhouse. There is a smash. Braino focuses on a hole in the greenhouse.

Braino No!

Moutho I told you.

Tummo Look what she's done.

Artlungs Are you sure she did it and not Our Boy?

Braino Are you suggesting I was responsible for that?

Artlungs No, Brain. Of course not . . .

Moutho Look!

Screen – Mudge's point of view. A Man's head pops up beside the greenhouse.

Man Who did that?

Screen – Mudge's point of view. Swings round to face Tidge. She smiles and says –

Tidge He did. That boy threw it.

Screen – Mudge's point of view. Turns back to face the Man, who climbs over the wall.

Man Right, you little devil, wait till I get hold of you.

Braino Say it wasn't us.

Moutho (*into microphone*) It wasn't us.

Man Think I'm going to believe that! Come here.

Tummo What do we do now?

Braino Run! Go into overdrive, Art! Warp Factor. Run!

Screen – Mudge's point of view. Starts running.

Moutho (*shouting into exit*) Get those lips open. Need more air.

Tummo (*to Artlungs*) Go faster.

Artlungs I am!

Tummo Mr M! Over here.

Tummo and Mr Memory help Artlungs move his legs faster.

Braino Automatic pilot.

The Screen goes off.
Braino dashes down to help move the pumps faster.
They are all belting away at the pumps. and do not
notice Germ who arrives from the stomach entrance.
He looks briefly at the Bods, studies the console, sniffs
dismissively and hides.
Lights down.
Lights up inside Tidge's head.
Screen – Tidge's point of view. Mudge is chased by
the Man. The Man stops. Tidge approaches.

Brainia That was a terrible thing to do!

Mouthia It was brilliant.

Tummia Pity he didn't catch him.

Mouthia It's not over yet. We're not far from school, are
we, Memory?

Ms Memory Just round the corner.

Screen – Tidge's point of view. The Man is panting in
front of her.

Man He a friend of yours.

Mouthia (*into microphone*) No sir. He's well known as
being a naughty boy. But I'm afraid he's in my class. (*to
Brainia*) Cry!

Brainia What?

Mouthia Come on, let's have some tears.

Brainia I –

Ms Memory I'll do it.

Mouthia (*into microphone*) I can never seem to get any
work done with him there.

Ms Memory Tears are go.

Man There, there, don't cry. He's gone.

Mouthia (*into microphone*) But he's always doing things like that.

Man Is he now? Which school do you go to?

Mouthia (*into microphone*) Round the corner.

Man Right, I'll be in to see your headteacher about that boy.

Tummia Great!

Man There, here's 50p. Buy yourself some chocolate.

Mouthia (*into microphone*) Thank you, sir.

> *Screen – Tidge's point of view. The Man goes off. Tidge walks towards school.*

Ms Memory Tears are stop. Automatic pilot.

> *Screen goes off.*

Tummia 50p, and that awful boy in trouble.

Mouthia Brilliant start to the day.

Ms Memory Don't you agree, Brain?

Brainia I think you're all disgusting. And one shouldn't take money from strangers.

Ms Memory What do you know? You're just a Brain. You're not smart.

Mouthia Or polite.

Tummia Or pretty.

All So there.

> *Lights down.*

Voice Over
    And so we move on into school where Mudge
      and Tidge await their test;
    But all's not well inside our boy, he isn't feeling
      at his best. *and the headteacher can*
                                      listen in

Lights up in Mudge's head.

Braino So, Mr Memory, I hope you're ready for this, or is
Our Boy to be faced with humiliation?

Mr Memory I'm going to need all the help I can get from
you lot.

Artlungs I'm not helping. I've just had to pump up for a
big run and quite frankly that's all I should be asked to do
for a bit.

Moutho Art.

Artlungs What?

Moutho Are you all right?

Artlungs Apart from . . . yes, of course.

Moutho You look exhausted.

Artlungs I said I was.

Tummo I'm not feeling too great.

Mr Memory Nor me. Excuse me, there's a file on river
pollution I need to check.

    Mr Memory goes.

Braino We know why you aren't feeling – (*He slips on the
steps as he starts to follow Mr Memory.*)

Moutho Brain, you just fell over.

Braino I know.

Tummo (*falls on the floor groaning*) Aaargh.

Moutho Tum.

Emergency lights flash.

Braino Emergency. Automatic pilot can't cope. Hands on control.

They stumble to their posts.

Moutho What is it?

Braino It's Miss. Screen On.

Screen – Mudge's point of view. Teacher is angrily standing over Mudge.

Volume up.

Teacher Go on then, Mudge. You don't want to keep the Head waiting –

Moutho (*into microphone*) No, Miss.

Teacher Or the gentleman whose greenhouse you used as target practice.

Screen – Mudge's point of view. Looks beyond the Teacher at a smirking Tidge.

Now!

Moutho (*into microphone*) But I –

Teacher The Head wants to see you now.

Moutho (*into microphone*) Yes, Miss.

Screen – Mudge's point of view. Walks towards the door.

Braino Nasty little cow.

Moutho Kick her as we go past.

Braino Too late. We've gone past her. Should have thought of that earlier.

Screen – Mudge's point of view. Walks down the corridor.

Tummo We always get the blame.

Moutho Never Miss Goody-Goody.

Braino We're here.

Screen – Mudge's point of view. Knocks on a door marked Headteacher. Head pokes his/her head round the door.

Head Oh. It's you, is it? Wait there.

Screen – Mudge's point of view. Door closes.

Braino Right. Automatic pilot.

Screen off.

Council of War. What do we say?

He slips again as he comes down.

Tummo The way I feel I couldn't care less at the moment.

Artlungs Or me.

Moutho What's happening to you all?

Braino I'm . . . I'm not sure. But I can't seem to stand up straight.

Germ enters.

Germ Maybe I can enlighten you.

Moutho Who are you?

Germ Can't you guess? Cigarette anyone? A finger of whisky?

Tummo groans. Braino struggles to his podium.

Braino White Corpuscles to the bridge. White Corpuscles to the bridge. This is an emergency.

Moutho You're an infection.

Germ Quite so. You've got problems haven't you? Accused of smashing a greenhouse and about to fail a test all in one day, Dear Boy. We are inside a boy, aren't we?

Braino Of course.

Germ Thought so. Difficult to know sometimes, when you come in through the mouth. No significant structural differences to observe.

Two White Corpuscles enter, kitted out like riot police.

Ah! These'll be your White Corpuscles! So aggressive.

White Corpuscle 1 What's up, Boss.

Braino Infection. Can you deal with it?

Germ stays cool as the White Corpuscles beat their sticks in their palms.

Now, please!

White Corpuscle 1 Infection, eh?

Braino What does it look like?

White Corpuscle 1 What does it look like to you, Dave?

White Corpuscle 2 There are infections and infections, Des.

White Corpuscle 1 And I'd call this a 'not something quite in our line sort of infection', Dave.

Braino What?

White Corpuscle 1 See, guvnor. Thing is, we White Corpuscles, we're basically bloodstream.

White Corpuscle 2 Splinters –

White Corpuscle 1 Grazes –

White Corpuscle 2 Nail in your hand –

White Corpuscle 1 Verruca –

White Corpuscle 2 Oh yes. Nothing like a nice verruca to get your teeth into.

White Corpuscle 1 What you've got here is more your Germ, I'd say.

Germ I prefer 'Virus'.

White Corpuscle 2 See. La-di-da.

White Corpuscle 1 And I'd bet you didn't get in through a hole in the skin, did you?

Germ Certainly not.

White Corpuscle 1 You'll have been ingested or inhaled.

Germ Ingested.

White Corpuscle 1 So, guv, not exactly our problem. Over to you. Ta-ta.

Braino What?

White Corpuscle 1 We'll be off then.

White Corpuscle 2 Nice meeting you.

They shake hands with Germ.

White Corpuscle 1 Good to meet the opposition off duty so to speak.

White Corpuscle 2 (*looks around at Tummo*) We'd best be getting back to base.

White Corpuscle 1 Might get lively here soon.

White Corpuscle 2 Get our seat belts on.

White Corpuscle 1 We'll waive the call-out charge this time.

Braino Oh, push off then.

White Corpuscle 1 Any more of that attitude, Brainy, old pal, and we'll stop working on that grazed knee you got last time Our Boy played football.

White Corpuscle 2 And then we'll be talking 'infection' with a capital 'I'.

White Corpuscle 1 Seepage.

White Corpuscle 2 Pus.

White Corpuscle 1 Oozing and –

White Corpuscle 2 Going yellow and green and –

Braino We get the point.

White Corpuscle 1 Still. Don't want to hang around here.

White Corpuscle 2 (*looking at Tummo again*) Yes. Let's be off sharpish. I really don't like the look of old Tum Tum over there.

> The White Corpuscles leave. Tapping bits of console and shaking their heads.

Moutho We ate you?

Germ I'm afraid so.

Braino When?

Germ Last night. I've been down in his Tummy Department wreaking havoc ever since.

Tummo groans.

Moutho Were you in the apple crumble?

Germ Good Lord, no. Remember those Smarties?

Braino I knew it.

Germ I wasn't in a Smarty, exactly, but they did fall out of the packet, didn't they!

Moutho Yes.

Germ And I've been lurking in the dust of your trouser pocket for weeks. All sorts of us down there, by the way, made great chums with a particularly virulent ear infection. I'll introduce you if you like. No? Fair enough. Anyway, eventually I latched on to a Smarty, a pink one to be precise, got popped through your lips by an appallingly grubby finger and thumb, then straight down while you were playing draughts with the Smarty I'd hitched a lift on. And that, my friends, is why you're not feeling so good. And may I say there's nothing you can do about it till I decide to go.

Braino Oh isn't there?

Braino lunges at Germ, who neatly flattens him.

Germ You'll have to do better than that, old thing.

Emergency lights flash.

Braino Screen on. Hands on control.

Screen – Mudge's point of view. Headteacher has opened the door and Mudge enters the office.

Head Sit down there, Mudge.

Screen – Mudge's point of view. Sits down. Head goes to a filing cabinet.

Germ You're in trouble now.

Braino We don't need you to tell us. Let me think.

Germ (*goes up to Moutho*) I tell you what . . . It gets a bit boring in the bottom of a pocket with all the other germs and bits of fluff, waiting for the odd Smarty to turn up. If I do you a favour, can I stay a day or so longer than usual? It's not a bad billet this.

Moutho What sort of favour?

Germ Get you off the test today. Give your Memory time to get his act together.

Mr Memory overhears this and nods frantically.
Screen – Mudge's point of view. Head returns to the desk with a file.

Moutho Okay. Brain, do as he says.

Braino What?

Moutho Now. Don't argue.

Braino I –

Germ Close your boy's eyes. Go on.

Moutho Go on, Brain.

Braino Why?

Moutho Just do it.

Braino Harrumph. This'd better work.

He switches a switch and the screen goes blank.

Germ (*to Moutho*) Grab his feet.

He grabs Tummo's shoulders. Moutho holds his feet.

Now, swing.

They swing a groaning Tummo from side to side.

Braino Stop it!

The lights flicker. Everybody is ill and moaning by now.

Germ Open the eyes!

Braino does so.
      Screen – Mudge's point of view. The picture is out of focus and wiggly. The Headteacher is leaning over the desk.

Head (*distorted voice*) Mudge. Mudge. Are you all right, Mudge?

Braino Oh no.

Germ Oh yes. How are you feeling, Tum?

Tummo I'm . . . I'm going to be –

Braino We're not.

Germ Oh yes, you are. You are going to be very, very, very sick.

Violent noises and distortions of light. The Bods fall all over the place.
      Screen – Mudge's point of view. The Headteacher reels back in horror, hands covered in green vomit. Mudge's eyes look down at a pool of sick on the desk. The Bods lie exhausted.

(*surveying the exhausted Bods*) There you are, boys. I told you I'd get you out of that test.

Act Two

Voice Over
   The Germ has had his wicked way.
   Our Boy is ill, but feels a fool,
   He isn't missing any school,
   He's missing play – it's Saturday
   When he plays football as a rule.

   Lights up in Mudge's head.
      Screen – Mudge's point of view. Lying in bed.
   Reading 'The Numbskulls'.
      Germ coolly surveys his wicked work. The Bods are
   slumped and listless.

Braino Next picture.

   Screen – Mudge's point of view. Moves on to next
   picture in the comic strip.

And the next.

   Screen – Mudge's point of view. Moves on to next
   picture in the comic strip.

Look, is anybody watching this?

Moutho No, it's rubbish.

Tummo Not true to life at all.

Braino Then it's going off if nobody's watching.

Germ I am.

Braino Huh! Screen off.

Screen goes off.

Moutho How long do you plan to stay?

Germ That depends.

Moutho On what?

Germ On how long I choose to stay. I like it here. Life of Riley. And none of you can do anything about it.

Tummo Oh yes we can.

Tummo nods at Moutho. Tummo goes for Germ. Germ flicks him off with nonchalant ease.

Germ Pathetic.

Moutho goes for him. He ends up in a heap too.

Look at you all. I tell you, when you've been in as many bodies as I have you get to know what's what.

Moutho And what's what with us?

Germ Take him for a start.

Artlungs What about me?

Germ How do you get on with Tum here?

Germ leans back and enjoys the squabbling as it rises in a crescendo of ill-feeling.

Artlungs Yuk.

Tummo Feeling's mutual.

Artlungs It's your fault he's here.

Moutho Don't you get at my mate.

Artlungs Two of a kind you are.

Moutho And so what?

Tummo Rather be my kind and living at the bottom of a toilet than your kind and . . .

Artlungs And what?

Tummo And not living there . . . I don't know.

Moutho Right.

Braino Leave Art alone, I want a council of war.

Moutho Bod off, Brain.

Tummo We're going to duff over Art here.

Braino Stop it.

Tummo And if you get in the way –

Moutho We'll duff you too.

Tummo So –

Braino Get off me.

Artlungs And me.

Tummo and Moutho are about to duff up Braino and Artlungs. Artlungs gets off his machine. In slow motion the others plonk him back then collapse in a heap.

Germ Do you think all bodies behave like that? You're a shambles. (*Germ sits up in Braino's console.*)

Braino We can work together when we need to.

Germ Can you?

Braino Of course we can.

Germ How old's your boy?

Braino Nearly twelve.

Germ Thought so. They stopped making this model just

after your boy was born.

Moutho Did they?

Germ Yes. Some of the babies I do these days have got computerised controls, databases, dot matrix fingerprinting, you name it. Of course, it's all digital.

Moutho What about grown-ups?

Germ Not me. My dad does them. He's brilliant. Put half of Barnsley in bed last winter with gastro-enteritis. Won Germ of the Year at the National Virus Awards.

Moutho Gosh.

Germ Takes years of experience to do grown-ups. Oh yes. My little brother tried it, you know. Just once. It was awful.

Tummo What happened?

Germ He was only a tiny apprentice germ at the time and he saw this man with a big beard and thought, 'I'll crawl up that and pop in his mouth and . . . ' Well, he got half way up, in sight of the chin, got tangled and didn't have the strength to get any further and –

Tummo And what? Go on. We like stories.

Germ Well he just got stuck. He survived on the odd bit of fried egg that came his way but . . . You know he survived for six months!

Tummo And then what?

Germ Then this chap washed his beard at last. Shampoo, conditioner, the lot; but my brother was so weak by then that he drowned in the cold water rinse. The man flicked his lifeless body out with a comb and he got squashed flat by the wheel of a passing baby buggy.

Moutho How sad.

Artlungs He should have tried getting in through his ear.

Germ His ear! Grown-ups have hair in their ears too! And if you get caught in that, they're likely to poke their finger in and flick you across the room on a lump of wax. I mean, lads, do grown-ups ever listen to what you say?

Moutho Never.

Germ Oh, they do. They listen but they don't hear. Because even if what you say gets through all that hair and wax, it gets all jumbled up in dust and cobwebs and filth. Not to mention the bits of old food hanging about because they haven't got enough teeth left to chew with and no one to tell them to brush their teeth properly.

And their burps! Yuk. See, because grown-ups think it's not polite to burp in public, if they feel a burp coming up they hold it at the top of their mouth, their eyes roll and they let it out bit by bit so no one hears. The smell inside their heads hangs around like boiled cabbage in the dinner hall on a wet Thursday.

And as for grown-ups that smoke! Inside them it's all brown and stained and peeling and musty. When smoking grown-ups cough, lumps of goo and glup slither up from their lungs into the back of their mouths and, unless they can have a good spit, they have to roll it all around and swallow it down again. Being inside a grown-up's no fun. And mark my words, the way you are at the moment, you"ll be in that sort of state sooner rather than later.

Tummo Oh no we won't.

Moutho Never.

Artlungs Urgh!

Germ Oh yes. You think you're in a mess – but it gets

worse, believe me.

Tummo So it's no fun being a Germ?

Germ You get to travel. See the world. But as soon as you start making friends, like with you lot, you have to move on.

Braino So you never stay long?

Germ No. I'm only a two-day bug. If you want the real McCoy, two weeks off and visits from the doctor, you'd have to get my dad.

Moutho Your mum a germ too?

Germ Yes. She's a Measle germ. You had Measles yet?

Tummo Mr Memory. Have we had Measles yet?

Mr Memory (*looking up from his studies*) No.

Germ You might get to meet her then.

Mr Memory I mean. I don't think so. We might have. Yes, I think so.

Germ She's German, my mum.

Tummo A German Measle!

Germ Not just your run of the mill, ordinary type.

Mr Memory I don't think we've had German Measles . . . Or, maybe . . . I . . . (*to himself*) Istanbul is now St Petersburg and it used to be Constantinople and before that it was Leningrad and . . . oh dear.

Germ He's keen. Not all Memories you meet are that studious.

Braino Too little too late. He's just a dreamer. No use to boy nor bod.

Moutho We're lucky you turned up. Getting us out of that test.

Tummo Saved our bacon.

Moutho Thanks.

Germ That's nice. Can't tell you how it warms the cockles to be appreciated once in a while.

Moutho See, Mr Memory can't remember anything.

A loud voice breaks through.

The Mum Mudge. Mudge. Are you all right?

Moutho It's The Mum.

Germ What do I do?

Braino You don't do anything. Get away from my Brainbox!

Germ What happens if I do this?

He presses a knob.

The Mum Mudge . . . oh no.

Braino gets up on his podium and takes control.

Braino Screen on. Idiot, you pressed the dribble button.

Artlungs Urgh. We're dribbling.

Screen – Mudge's point of view. In bed. The Mum is wiping his face with a tissue. Moutho goes to his microphone.

Moutho (*into microphone*) Sorry, Mum. I was just dozing.

The Mum How are you feeling?

Moutho (*into microphone*) Bit better.

NON-TRANSFERABLE BETWEEN VEHICLES

Refund of Vehicle Tax

If you want to apply for a refund
of vehicle tax you will need to fill in a
V14 application form which you can get from
www.direct.gov.uk/motoringforms
any Post Office® branch that issues tax discs
or in Northern Ireland at any DVA local office.

Tummo No we're not.

Braino Oh no!

Screen – Mudge's point of view. Behind The Mum we see that Tidge has followed her into the room.

Tummo What's she doing here?

Moutho I don't know. (*into microphone*) What's she doing here, Mum?

The Mum I've got to pop out to the shops. Tidge said she'd sit here and cheer you up.

Moutho (*into microphone*) She won't –

Tidge Yes, I will.

Screen – Mudge's point of view. Tidge sits down by the bed.

The Mum (*going*) Good girl. I won't be long. Tidge'll get you anything you need.

Screen – Mudge's point of view. The Mum goes and Tidge smiles evilly.

Germ That girl's up to no good.

Braino What do we do?

Moutho Pretend Our Boy's asleep.

Braino Eyes shut.

Screen off.

Tummo Press the snore button.

Braino It only works if we're really asleep.

Moutho I'll do pretend snore. (*into microphone*) Cor phew, cor phew –

They all start shaking about as though in an earthquake.

Braino She's shaking us. Hang on.

Germ Haven't you got stabilisers?

Braino They're on the blink because of you.

Germ Sorry.

Tummo Keep pretending. She'll get fed up in a minute.

Tidge Mudge, Mudge, Mudge.

Lights down – 'Mudge, Mudge, Mudge' echoes on and on.
   Lights up inside Tidge's head.
   Screen – Tidge's point of view. Shaking Mudge.

Mouthia (*into microphone*) Mudge, Mudge, Mudge.

Tummia He's not really asleep.

Ms Memory I know. Keep shaking him.

Mouthia No! Stop shaking. Eyes right.

Screen – Tidge's point of view. She stops shaking and looks at glass of water on bedside table.

This'll wake him up.

Brainia We mustn't.

Mouthia Pick it up.

Tummia (*goes over to Brainia's podium*) Go on. Or I'll pinch your legs. Like that. Only harder.

Brainia manipulates her controls and:
   Screen – Tidge's point of view. The hand picks up the water and pours it over Mudge's head.
   The Bodettes laugh uproariously.

Mudge What did you do that for?

Mouthia (*into microphone*) We haven't got much time before your Mummy comes back.

Mudge What for?

Mouthia (*into microphone*) To tell you about the test.

Mudge What about it?

Mouthia (*into microphone*) We all did it. You've got to do it on Monday. Do you want to know the answers?

> *Lights down – 'The answers', 'The answers' echoes round.*
> *Lights up in Mudge's head.*
> *Screen – Mudge's point of view. Tidge leaning over him.*

Tidge So, do you? Do you want to know the answers?

Braino Say yes.

Moutho I don't trust her.

Braino Mr Memory, get ready. She's going to tell us the geography answers.

Tummo What do you think?

Germ Not my problem. I'll be well gone by Monday.

Braino Say yes –

Moutho (*into microphone*) Okay, what are they?

> *Lights down – 'What are they?' 'What are they?' echoes around.*
> *Lights up inside Tidge's head*
> *Screen – Tidge's point of view. Mudge interested.*

Mudge Come on then, what are they?

Mouthia He's fallen for it.

Brainia This is awful. We shouldn't be doing this.

Tummia I know. Isn't it great.

Mouthia First one, Ms Memory?

Ms Memory The first question was about that map of the British Isles.

Mouthia (*into microphone*) The first question was about the British Isles.

> *Lights down – 'British Isles', 'British Isles' echoes about.*
> *Lights up in Mudge's head. Mr Memory is taking notes.*
> *Screen – Mudge's point of view. Tidge by the bed.*

Tidge And you had to recognise mountain ranges and rivers and put cities in.

Artlungs I could do that.

Tummo (*threatens him*) Stick a cork in it, Art.

Braino Get this down, Mr Memory.

Tidge Up at the top in Scotland there are some mountains called the Pennines.

Moutho (*into microphone*) Pennines.

> *Screen – Mudge's point of view. Tidge nods.*

Artlungs I knew that.

Tidge And two big cities. Cardiff and Dublin.

Mr Memory Cardiff and Dublin.

Tidge Cardiff in the West and Dublin in the East.

Braino Got that?

Mr Memory I'm not sure about –

Braino Just write it down. What are you all gawping at? Get on with what you're supposed to be doing. Mr M, come up here. Screen off. Private listening.

Screen goes off.
   Mr Memory looks pleadingly at the others but starts taking notes at the console. Germ beckons Moutho over to where Tummo is still standing over Artlungs.

Artlungs Urgh. Don't come over here, nasty germ.

Moutho What do you think?

Germ You are being fed misinformation.

Tummo I knew it.

Artlungs No you didn't.

Germ Dublin! I've been there inside a little girl. On a ferry! The sea was so rough she didn't need my help. So Dublin's in Ireland, not Scotland.

Moutho You're sure.

Germ Positive.

Tummo So what do we do?

Germ I've got an idea. It's worked before. Interested?

Tummo and Moutho Yes.

Germ But you two can't help, I mean, you can help, but for my plan to work I really need him and him (*indicating Braino and Mr Memory*).

Lights down.

Voice Over
  Germ tells the Bods of the plot he's planned,
  This plan he's plotted, through and through.
  And all the while Tidge carries on
  And on with facts that just aren't true.

Lights up in Tidge's head.
  Screen – Tidge's point of view. Mudge listening intently and then looking increasingly blank.
  Brainia is angrily confined to her chair. Mouthia, prompted by Ms Memory, spouts facts into the microphone. Tummia is keeping an eye on Brainia.

Mouthia (*into microphone*) And the River Thames is the longest river in . . . the world.

Tummia That's going too far. He'll never believe that.

Screen – Tidge's point of view. Mudge nods distantly.

Ms Memory He has.

They cheer.

Tummia Isn't he so stupid?

Ms Memory There was that question on volcanoes. Tell him volcanoes are caused by people digging holes in the ground and lighting the coal, which explodes.

Moutho Right.

Tummia Hold on. I don't think he's listening any more.

Screen – Tidge's point of view. Mudge has gone very blank.

Ms Memory He does look strange.

Moutho (*into microphone*) Mudge. Mudge. Mudge.

Lights down – 'Mudge', 'Mudge', 'Mudge' echoes about.

Lights up in Mudge's head. Braino and Mr Memory are being dressed as germs.

Braino I am not doing it.

Moutho Yes, you are.

Braino Can't Mr Memory go on his own?

Moutho No. It'll need two of you to cover him.

Artlungs While he what? What's happening?

Moutho Germ's taking Mr M and Brain into that girl's head to loot her memory banks.

Braino But why me? I'm needed here.

Germ No you're not. Your Boy's ill in bed. These three can look after things while we're away. And you might very well be needed over there.

Braino But –

Germ If we get there and she gets bored and wants to go, we'll have to take over and need someone brave, resourceful, clever and skilled to drive her close to Your Boy so you and Mr M can get back on board.

Braino Me. Brave?

Germ Yes.

Braino Clever?

Germ And skilled.

Braino I say.

Moutho We'll just keep Our Boy here in bed. So it's going to be up to you to get back on board when you can.

Braino No tampering with my Brain Box.

Tummo No, Brain.

Braino Right. Let's go.

Mr Memory How do we get there?

Braino Er . . .

Germ There's kissing.

Tummo Kissing, yuk.

Germ Usually works.

Artlungs Oh yes, let's try that.

Germ Or there's the sneeze.

Moutho Great idea. How do you do a sneeze, Brain?

Braino It's that button but you need maximum tickle pressure in the lungs.

They look at Artlungs.

Artlungs Oh no.

Tummo I'll do that.

Germ Good. Now we'll all have to cling to each other. Sneezes can be random and you don't want to drown in that vase of daffodils.

Braino, Germ and Mr Memory cling on to each other near the entrance to the mouth.

Moutho All ready?

Germ Ready, sir.

Moutho Build windpipe tickle pressure, Tum.

Artlungs No.

Tummo Pressure building.

He starts tickling Artlungs who starts laughing and pedalling faster and faster.

Moutho Quarter pressure.

Braino You need more than that.

Moutho Half pressure.

Germ Hold tight, chaps.

Lights down – The amplified sound of Artlungs giggling.
  Lights up in Tidge's head.
  Screen – Tidge's point of view. Mudge is building up to a sneeze.

Mouthia Something's up.

Tummia You don't think he's going to be sick like he was over the headmaster.

Ms Memory Doesn't look like that to me.

Brainia Do you want me to tell you what it is?

Tummia How would you know?

Brainia shrugs.

Mouthia Do you know?

Brainia Yes.

Tummia Then tell us.

Brainia Sure you want to know.

Mouthia Come on, you stupid Brain.

Brainia He's going to sneeze.

Screen – Tidge's point of view. Mudge sneezes right in her face.

Screen goes blank.
The Bodettes collapse as Germ, Braino and Mr
Memory leap into their head.

Germ On guard! Take the bridge.

Braino (*to Brainia*) Off there!

Brainia No. Help me!

They struggle for control of the brain box.
Only Brainia shows any resistance. The other Bodettes
cower and whimper. Braino takes control of the
console.

Braino Enemy Brain Box captured, Sir! Right. Automatic
pilot. No move status. Screen on.

Screen – Tidge's point of view. Mudge lying back on the
pillows looking blank.

All in order, sir.

Germ Screen off, Number One.

Braino Screen off.

Screen goes off. The Bodettes are shepherded together.

Germ So, my pretty ones, what sort of craft have we
ventured aboard?

The other Bodettes push Brainia forward.

Brainia A girl.

Germ And do you know who we are?

Brainia I presume you're Germs.

Braino We prefer 'Virus'.

Brainia Whatever you are, get out of this body. Now.

Germ I'm Captain Gastro-Enteritis. This is my first mate, Dicky Tummy and . . .

Mr Memory has wandered over to inspect the Artlungs machine.

Braino (*whisper*) Mr M, pay attention!

Brainia Mr Who?

Braino Er . . .

Germ Mr Embiotic Viral Infection. We call him Mr M for short.

Mr Memory Look at this, Brai –

Braino Dicky! Remember, I'm your old friend, Dicky Tummy?

Mr Memory But look!

They gaze at the Artlungs machine's automatic pedalling system.

Braino Okay! Where is she?

Brainia Who?

Braino Your Artlungs, who do you think?

Mouthia What's he talking about?

Germ Hold hard, Dicky Tummy, old shipmate. Belay there.

Braino What?

Germ How old's this girl we're in?

Ms Memory Eleven years and one month.

Germ (*to Braino*) She's the 1989 model. Your . . . that boy we were just in, he's the 1988 model. Too early for the Automatic Artlungs Modification.

Tummia You were in that Mudge boy.

Braino Certainly were, sister.

Mouthia So you were the germs –

Braino Viruses, please.

Brainia Germs!

Mouthia Who made him sick?

Tummia Over the Headmaster.

Braino The very team.

Tummia starts crying.

Germ That's enough Mr Nice Guy, my viral compadres . . . You! That one there. You remembered how old your girl was. Are you in charge of the Memory Banks.

Ms Memory Yes, sir.

Germ And where, pray, do you keep them?

Ms Memory Round there, sir.

Germ Good. Mr Embiotic Viral Infection –

Mr Memory Me?

Germ You, me and our new acquaintance of a memorial disposition here are going to take a little look-see. Walk.

Ms Memory goes. Mr Memory and Germ follow her off.

Dicky Tummy –

Braino Sir!

Germ Keep a tight ship while we're gone.

Braino Aye, aye, sir. (*He strides about looking threatening.*)

Braino Sit down all of you.

Mouthia and Tummia sit.

Brainia You really a germ?

Braino I am, and I'm going to make you suffer or my name's not Dicky Tummy.

Brainia Then how come you're not familiar with an Automatic Artlungs.

Braino I . . . I usually do older people, grown-ups, I'm new to children's work.

Brainia Most germs we've had have been special children's germs. Haven't they?

Mouthia and Tummia nod in a frightened manner.

Braino Well. Now you know what a proper grown-up Germ is like. Grrrrr.

Brainia You're no Germ.

Braino Sit down right now. Or things'll look ugly for you, my hearty. Very ugly. (*He struts about, casting furtive glances towards the Memory exit.*)

Tummia (*whispering*) Why are you trying to make things worse?

Brainia He's not a Germ.

Mouthia What do you know?

Brainia I know that for once in Our Girl's life we've got to work together.

Tummia But they're stronger than us.

Mouthia And although we're smart –

Tummia And polite –

Mouthia And pretty –

Brainia Oh, what's the point? You are pathetic. I know how we can get out of this. Will you stop being so mimsy and take a chance?

Tummia I . . .

Mouthia I suppose so.

Brainia Good. Now, Tummy, remember what you had for lunch just now?

Tummia Spaghetti.

Brainia Exactly. Now this is what I want you to do.

Lights down – 'Want you to do, want you to do'
echoes over the fold back.
   Lights up in Mudge.

Tummo Wonder how they're getting on.

Moutho Have a look.

Tummo Can I?

Moutho If you like.

Artlungs Don't let him near that brain box.

Moutho It's third lever on the left. Now you push that and say 'Screen on'.

Screen – Mudge's point of view. Looking at a troubled
Tidge.

Hey, this is great.

Moutho She doesn't look very happy.

Tummo Does that mean it's working?

Moutho Maybe. Lean closer. Look into her eyes, we

might be able to spot them.

Artlungs Then we can all wave, I suppose. Tut.

Tummo Leaning forward? Leaning . . . Is that it?

Screen – Mudge's point of view. The picture tilts sideways looking at the wall.

Moutho No. Try that one.

Screen – Mudge's point of view. Looks at the ceiling.

Give it here.

Tummo No! It's my go!

Lights down – 'My go', 'My go', 'My go' echoes round the fold back.
Lights up in Tidge's head.
Brainia looks cool. Mouthia and Tummia huddle behind her. Braino is desperately hoping for the others to come back. Brainia nudges Tummia.

Brainia Now.

Tummia starts to groan and writhe about.

Braino What's up with her?

Brainia You're the Germ. You tell us.

Braino Oh. Yes. She's your Tummy, isn't she. See, I've given her Dicky Tummy. Ha, ha! Writhe, writhe. Agony, agony. Ha, ha!

Brainia I'd better pass the word through the rest of the body.

Braino What!

Brainia Let everybody know what's happening.

Braino Stay here.

Brainia (*going to the mouth entrance*) I'm not going anywhere. (*Shouts.*) Everybody! We've got a tummy bug. We can't beat it, it's too strong. Really tough, terrifying germs. Sorry, they were too good for us.

Braino looks smug. Brainia suddenly swings round with a long strand of spaghetti. She flings the end at Mouthia.

Grab it. Now, go!

They run round Braino and wind him up like a cocoon, then tie a neat bow in the end.

You get more. I'll wait there.

Mouthia and Tummia dash off.

Germ (*off*) What's all that shouting, Dicky?

Germ and the two Memories return. Mr Memory is carrying files.

Mr Memory I've got it all, Brain.

Brainia Now!

Mouthia and Tummia run out with spaghetti strands and wrap Mr Memory up while Brainia leaps on Germ. Germ shakes her off. They warily circle each other.

Right, girls. Remember what I said. Work together and we'll get him.

Germ Brave words, girlie!

Brainia So you're the only real Germ!

Germ And I've never lost a fight in my life.

Brainia There's always a first time, even for a Gastric Gadfly.

Germ Fine sentiments, my saucy cerebellum. Choose

your weapons!

Brainia I choose more spaghetti! But you can't have any.

Germ That's not fair.

Brainia Our head. Our rules, Germy.

*They all fight. Brainia marshals her troops and they
wrap Germ up.*

So! As I said there's always a first time. Now, who just are
you?

*Lights down. 'Who are you', 'Who are you', 'Who are
you?' echoes round.*
    Lights up in Mudge's head.
    *Tummo and Moutho are still trying to figure the
controls. They jolt from side to side.*

Moutho What are you doing? It's this one.

Tummo No it's not. I've already tried that. It's –

They lurch.

Artlungs Don't argue about it, just find it.

They lurch.

Moutho This! Now – screen on! I said, 'Screen on'.

Tummo Try that. Screen on!

*Screen goes on – Mudge's point of view. Tidge and the
bedroom lurching from side to side.*

Tummo Nya, nya.

Moutho So clever clogs, how do you stop –

They lurch.

That!

Tummo Get away from my Brain Box and I'll show you.

Moutho *Your* Brain Box?

Tummo Go on. Shoo.

Moutho (*going over to Artlungs*) Who does he think he is?

Tummo There. No more lurching. That's it!

Screen – Mudge's point of view. He is getting out of bed.

Artlungs What's happening now?

Moutho We're getting out of bed. Tum, you mustn't.

Tummo Easy, peasy. Just stretching Our Boy's legs a bit.

Artlungs Stop him.

Moutho Get Our Boy back to bed and get off there.

Tummo No.

Moutho Come on.

Tummo I've spent years waiting for this moment. And now I'm going to have fun.

Moutho But Tum!

Screen – Mudge's point of view. Walking about the room. Screen goes off.

Tummo Aargh! Lost it. Once we get to the kitchen, Our Boy will take his first great step to becoming a Tummy on legs.

Screen on – Mudge's point of view. Still in the room.

That's it. Now! Let's head for that door.

Screen – Mudge's point of view. Walks into a wall.

Screen goes blank.

Nyergh. Let's try these –

Moutho Don't, Tum, don't!

Tummo (*kicks him away*) 'Sir', if you please! Don't call me Tum any more. It's 'Mr Tum' or better still 'Sir'! Got that? You call me 'Sir'!

> *Lights down. Echoes of 'Call me sir', 'Call me sir'.*
>> *Lights up in Tidge's head.*
>> *Germ, Braino and Mr Memory are trussed up.*
> *Brainia is very much in charge.*

Brainia So, that was your pathetic, grubby little plan.

Tummia They were going to steal all our memory and cheat in the test?

Mouthia Disgusting. Dirty. Horrible –

Braino Only because you started telling us the wrong answers.

Tummia How do you know they're wrong?

Mr Memory Everybody knows Dublin's not in Scotland –

Tummia You didn't.

Braino Yes, we –

Brainia Stop it all of you! We've got to work out how to get them back to their Boy's body –

Mouthia No –

Brainia Yes. And we are going to do it now. Screen on!

> *Screen on – Tidge's point of view. An empty bed where Mudge should be.*

He's gone!

Braino He can't have.

Brainia Scan the room.

Screen – Tidge's point of view. Looking about the room. Mudge walks into a wall.

Tummia There he is.

Mouthia What's he doing?

Braino The idiots. They're playing with the controls.

Brainia Who are?

Screen – Tidge's point of view. Mudge changes direction and goes through the door.

Braino Tum, Mouth? I don't know. What do you think, Mr M?

Mr Memory If I could see properly I might be able to hazard a guess.

Brainia Untie them.

Mouthia What?

Brainia We might need their help. Untie them.

Ms Memory I'll untie you, Mr Memory.

Brainia Hold tight everybody. This is an emergency!

Lights down – 'This Is An Emergency' echoes round. Lights up in Mudge's head.
Screen – Mudge's point of view – in the hall heading for the kitchen.
Artlungs and Moutho are frightened. Tummo is in manic control.

Tummo So, what shall we tuck into first, my dearios. Fridge or larder. Cupboard or bread bin.

Screen – Mudge's point of view. Enters the kitchen.
The lights begin to flicker. A low, hollow, frightening sound gets louder through the scene.

What's that? Keep pumping, Art.

Artlungs I am. But we're losing power.

Tummo Now! Fridge first, I think.

Screen – Mudge's point of view. Lurches at the fridge. Opens it and grabs at a lump of cheese.

Moutho I think we've got a malfunction.

Tummo Be quiet and get down.

Moutho Are you keeping the brainwaves going?

Screen – Mudge's point of view. Fails to get a grip on the cheese.

Tummo You're distracting me.

Artlungs (*pumping furiously*) I don't think he is. I'm getting no power.

Moutho Switch the brainwaves on to automatic.

Tummo I want *cheese*!

Moutho (*clambering up*) Tum, you must or we'll –

Tummo Get off me.

The lights flicker badly. The hollow noise grows.
Artlungs pumps furiously. Tummo and Moutho wrestle for control of the console.
Explosion. Smoke and darkness. Tummo, Moutho and Artlungs scream in terror.
Lights down – screaming over the fold back.
Lights up in Tidge's head.

Screen – Tidge's point of view. Mudge walking out into the garden. He trips over. He goes into the street in his pyjamas. His face is blank as though all the lights have gone out inside him.

Brainia He's heading towards the road.

Braino They've broken him. They've broken Our Boy.

Mr Memory What's happened?

Braino It looks like the Brainwaves and Bodywaves have lost all coordination. Which means he's like a train going down a steep slope without any engines, any driver or . . . any brakes!

Brainia Call after him!

Mouthia (*into microphone*) Mudge! Mudge! Stop will you. Mudge!

Screen – Tidge's point of view. Mudge walks into the road and is nearly run down by a car.

Everyone Aaaaaah!

Brainia See what happens when other Bods meddle with the things they don't understand.

Screen – Tidge's point of view. Mudge carries on walking into the park towards a bench.

Mouthia We don't do that.

Tummia We certainly don't.

Ms Memory Yes, we do.

Mouthia and Tummia Memory!

Ms Memory We were talking back there, Mr Memory and I, and we both remembered that the times things go wrong are the times we don't all work together.

Mr Memory And when you, Brain –

Braino Me?

Ms Memory Or you, Tummy –

Tummia Me?

Mr Memory – Let us get on with things without nagging us, we both work quite well.

Ms Memory And we worked that out because –

Both Two memories are better than one.

> *They stand soppily holding hands.*

And we've worked out a plan of action.

Brainia Are you going to tell us what it is?

Ms Memory Say 'please'.

Brainia Please.

Mr Memory All of you say 'please'.

Everyone Please.

> *Screen – Tidge's point of view. Mudge sits on a bench. He picks up a discarded fast food chicken leg. He starts gnawing at it.*

Brainia Oh no. It's an old chicken leg.

Germ Lots of my pals on that I expect.

Ms Memory He's going to eat it. So it must be your Tum in charge, Mr Memory.

Mr Memory Good. Now while he's concentrating on that can we manoeuvre round behind.

Tummia Why?

Mr Memory Because if he sees Your Girl get close he might run away again.

Brainia Right. Moving behind him.

Screen – Tidge's point of view. Moves behind Mudge and slowly leans in towards his ear.

Germ At the right moment you two get to the back of the throat.

Braino And jump on the waggler.

Mouthia The what?

Tummia We haven't got one of those.

Mr Memory He means the uvula. Hey, I remembered what it's called!

Brainia Nearly there.

Braino I hope this works, Mr M.

Mr Memory You know as well as I do that if there's one thing Tum likes more than food it's my stories.

Braino I know that, but can you remember any of them?

Mr Memory 'Course I can.

Braino Then get on with it.

Mr Memory Give me a moment to think.

Braino We haven't got a mo –

Brainia Shush! Don't nag him.

Mr Memory I just need to do it in my own time.

Braino (*under his breath*) Hippy.

Mr Memory And with a little help from my friends.

He squeezes Ms Memory's hand. They smile even more soppily at each other.

Tummia (*to Mouthia*) What's a hippy?

Mouthia It's the bit at the top of the leggy.

Brainia Coming in close enough to start. Begin when you like.

Mr Memory Permission to use your vocal chords, Mouth?

Mouthia I – (*She looks at Brainia.*) I suppose so.

Mr Memory (*into microphone*) Tum. Can you hear me, Tum. I'm going to tell you a story. It's your favourite. About the boy. Listen carefully, Tum.

> As far away as a map can say,
> To the right of a town called Wrong,
> In a village as old as the snow is cold
> Was a boy who sang a haunting song.

Lights down.
   Grey light up in Mudge – the Bods are dazed and bewildered.

Tummo Chicken leg . . . chicken leg . . . chicken leg . . .

Moutho Listen.

Artlungs What?

Moutho That voice. It's Mr Memory. Telling his story.

Mr Memory's voice continues as a voice over. Tummo begins to listen.

Mr Memory
He lived alone in a house of stone
By a river that saw no sun,

And nobody knew a thing about who
He was or whence he'd come.

On a stool at his door, this pale-faced boy,
With eyes of emerald green,
While others played, he sang all the day
A song that grew out of his dreams.

Tummo is visibly moved by the story.

Tummo It's the boy, isn't it. My favourite story.

Moutho (*into microphone*) Keep going Mr Memory.

Mr Memory
It would start as a sigh, a mournful cry
With a chill that could torture the dead;
In a second it changed and a jaunty refrain 'd
Make your teeth dance a jig in your head.

Tummo They don't like him just because he's different . . .

Mr Memory
While other lads grew into muscular youths,
And believed they weren't scared any more;
This boy remained young and continued his song
On the stool, in the shade, at his door.

*Tummo is reduced to tears. Moutho comforts him.
They join in with bits of the story.*

Tummo Oh no. I know the three lads are going to –

Mr Memory
Then three youths feeling rash, bet each other
    in cash
They'd at last put a stop to his tune.
Their malevolent trick was to pelt him with
    bricks,

Stones and rocks, by the dark of the moon.
And then brick upon stone, the song sank to
    a moan
As his body lay battered and broken,
'Midst a pile of rock, while the village's clock
Struck thirteen to show Hatred had spoken.

And from that day to this, if a child wants to
    whistle
Or sing or share dreams from his head,
They'll be struck with a rod and told not to seem
    odd
For the last one to do that is dead.

*Braino and Mr Memory leap aboard. Braino rushes to
his brain box.*

Braino Mr M, help Art get pressure back.

Mr Memory Right, Brain.

Braino Brainwaves functioning. Bodywaves in
coordination. No sign of any lasting damage. Mouth, is
Tum all right?

Moutho He's fine. Just had a bit of a shock.

*The lights and Artlungs' power are getting back to
normal.*

Tummo Mr Memory, was that you?

Mr Memory 'Course it was.

Tummo How?

Braino Seventy per cent normal power.

Mr Memory I'm not sure, but it worked, didn't it?

Braino Eighty per cent.

Moutho But did you do it? Did you raid her Memory Banks?

Braino Ninety.

Mr Memory Yes. Oh yes we did. Brain, can we have the screen on, please?

Braino Not yet. Ninety-five per cent power.

Mr Memory Only I'd like to look into that girl's eyes and see if I can see her.

Tummo He's gone potty.

Moutho Mr M, are you all right?

Mr Memory Just want to say thank you.

Braino Hundred per cent. All systems functioning. No permanent damage. No defects. We have regained control.

The Bods cheer.
  Lights down – Cheers echo round.

Lights up in Tidge's head – The Bodettes watch the screen.
  Screen – Tidge's point of view. Mudge stands up.

Ms Memory Did you hear that?

Tummia What?

Ms Memory They're cheering. He's all right.

Tummia Wonder which 'he' she's talking about?

Mouthia As if it wasn't obvious.

Screen – Tidge's point of view. Mudge smiles at her.

Mudge Thanks.

Brainia Let's get him back to his house.

Mouthia (*into microphone*) Back home now, Mudge.

Screen – Tidge's point of view. Mudge nods and starts walking to the park gate.

Brainia Screen off. Well done, everybody. I think Our Girl should have a bar of chocolate to celebrate.

Mouthia Brain! We've told you before we don't do things like that. We're polite –

Tummia And we're pretty and –

Ms Memory I think a bar of chocolate's a good idea.

Mouthia and **Tummia** Memory!

Brainia Or maybe two. And a read of a comic.

Ms Memory And hours of watching television.

Brainia And Our Girl lounging about in bed in her nightie.

Ms Memory And another bar of chocolate.

Tummia We'd be sick.

Brainia Tummy, I'm afraid we've got no choice about that. There's a little blip on my Brain Box that says there's trouble down in your department –

Tummia There can't be.

Germ enters.

Germ I'm afraid there can. Nice clean patch you keep down there.

Tummia (*weakly*) Thank you.

Germ But I relish a challenge. However it's a little more comfy up here so . . . mind if I make this my corner?

Brainia Have we any choice?

Germ Not really. Now that I've had a chance to do my wicked work you're stuck with me. They play draughts in that boy. Got any Smarties?

Brainia We could buy some.

Ms Memory I'll play the winner.

Germ This could be fun. What comics does Your Girl read?

Tummia I don't feel well at all.

Germ Let's work out a timetable then. Now, you'll be sick in a couple of hours I'd say, so after that you won't feel too good but by tomorrow morning . . .

Lights down.

Voice Over
So Tidge's Bods have met the Germ, and make
the best of feeling bad.
Meanwhile that night in Mudge's head,
The Boy is tucked up warm in bed
And Brain's about to have his say about the day
they've had.

Lights up in Mudge.
Screen – Mudge's point of view – view from the bed.
The Mum about to kiss him goodnight.

Braino Mouth! Prepare for your department for a goodnight kiss with The Mum.

Moutho Yes, Brain.

The Mum Night, night, sleep tight, don't let the bugs bite.

Moutho (*into microphone*) Night, night, Mum.

Screen – Mudge's point of view. The Mum kisses him, turns off the light and goes out.

(*returning to Tummo*) She always says that. Tch!

Braino Brain Box off for the night. Screen going off. Automatic pilot. Sleeping mode. No alarm set. So-o-o. I think we'd all agree it's been a difficult day.

All Yes, Brain.

Braino But we've come through it.

All Yes, Brain.

Braino Some of us with honour . . . and some of us without honour.

Tummo Sorry, Brain.

Braino I warned that there'd be some changes round here, and so there shall be. Art, I promised you a change.

Artlungs Yes, friend.

Braino Tum, I think you know what I'm going to say.

Tummo Yes, Brain.

Tummo walks over to the pedal cycle and changes places with Artlungs who gets off but is unable to curb a pedalling style of walking. Brain is about to speak, but stops himself.

Artlungs Oh thank you, thank you. So Mr Memory'll take over from Tum and I can be the new Mr Memory?

Braino No. But there is a new job lined up for you.

Bottom Ender comes in looking as smart as he can.

Bottom Ender You buzzed for me, Brain?

Artlungs Oh no. Not the Bottom End. Not that.

Tummo Serves you right. Moan, moan, moan, all the time.

Artlungs Get off there. I'm still Artlungs. Anything but the –

Braino Silence. Bottom Ender. You take over the Art Lungs Department.

Bottom Ender Me? Artlungs?

Bottom Ender yanks Tummo off and starts pedalling.

Brilliant! Fresh air. Exercise. After years cooped up in the dark down there in the Nether Regions. Thank you, Brain.

Braino Tum.

Tummo Yes?

Braino I was talking to Tum.

Tummo But I'm –

Artlungs Me? Tum?

Braino Yes.

Tummo Which means –

Braino You'd best be off. Say hallo to your new department, 'Bottom Ender'.

Tummo But it's smelly and dark down there.

Bottom Ender You said you liked the smell.

Braino Off you go.

Artlungs Don't worry, I'll give you lots to do. From now on we'll only eat fresh fruit, vegetables. No more Smarties or crisps or –

Moutho Hold on. I ask for the things we eat, not you –

Artlungs I'm sure Brain agrees with me that a healthy, fibre-filled diet –

Tummo How long am I Bottom Ender for?

Braino We'll see.

Tummo Oh. Bye-bye, Mr Memory. Think of me.

Mr Memory It's very valuable work, Tum. And I'm sure you'll . . . er . . . enjoy it.

Tummo Hope so. (*to Moutho*) Sorry, I went funny. We're still mates, aren't we?

Moutho 'Course we are, Tum – I mean, Bum.

Tummo Good. I'll go then.

Braino Now.

Bottom Ender Don't worry, you soon get used to the atmosphere.

> *Tummo goes.*

Braino Good. That's done. Everybody happy? Lights out then. Let's get to sleep.

> *Lights go down. The Bods settle down.*

Bottom Ender The rest of you all go to sleep now, do you?

Artlungs Certainly do.

Bottom Ender But I don't?

Artlungs Nope.

Bottom Ender All right for some Bods. Pump, pump,

pump for me then, is it?

Artlungs 'Fraid so. Hee, hee.

Bottom Ender I picture this job becoming a trifle tedious after a while.

Moutho Put a sock in it, Art.

Pause.

Artlungs Mouth.

Moutho What, Art? I mean, 'Tum'.

Artlungs I'm not used to going to sleep. How do you do it?

Moutho It helps if you shut up for a start.

Artlungs Or if we're told a story?

Moutho Sometimes. Mr M?

Mr Memory What?

Moutho Can we have a story –

Mr Memory Not tonight. Brain might get upset.

Moutho Oh. Sorry. Don't want to upset Brain tonight of all nights, do we?

Artlungs Certainly not.

Braino I'd very much like to hear a story.

Mr Memory Would you?

Braino Yes, please.

Mr Memory Oh. Good. Here goes then.

Behind the eyes of every boy, between the ears
   of every girl,

Under your browns, above your nose is where
    you'll find another world.
A world of Bods who run your life; who fly you
    as you'd fly a plane,
From when you live to when you die, and
    Captain of them all is Brain.

Braino This sounds like a good story.

Bottom Ender Pump, pump, pump, pump.

*The lights fade. The gurglings of a body drown out
Bottom Ender's voice.*

ODESSA AND THE MAGIC GOAT

John Agard

My thanks to
Christopher Leith, Lindie Wright
and all of the Little Angels Theatre.
And, of course, to John Wright's puppets,
which inspired *Odessa and the Magic Goat*
J. A.

Characters

Narrator
Papa Puppeteer
Leopard
Goat
Ni-Ni
Sushay
Tasa
Odessa
Kaba

Act One

Narrator
Papa Puppeteer get ready your strings.
A story, a story of ancient things.
Maybe a dragon on flaming wings.
Maybe a fairy with a shining wand
To whisk us away to a faraway land.
We'll travel in water, we'll travel by air
As long as you promise you'll take us there.
We'll travel by plane, by train or by boat.
Or even on the back of a goat.

Papa Puppeteer
Did I hear you say
On the back of a goat?
I may be able to help you my friend.
I happen to know such a goat
But have you a goat-story to tell?

Narrator
Sure as I have a nose to smell
And ears to hear.
Sure as I can ring a bell
And breathe in air.
Sure as my belly has a button
And my toes have a corn.
Sure as lamb is to mutton
As goat is to horn
I've been telling stories
From the day I was born.

Papa Puppeteer
    Never mind your belly button,
    Never mind the smell in your nose,
    Never mind the corn on your toes,
    Never mind your ringing bell,
    Where is the story you promise to tell?

Narrator
    Where is the goat you said you knew?
    I'm waiting, so are all these children too.

Papa Puppeteer
    Grass to chew
    And hills to climb
    Horns on the head
    And a tail behind.
    Come on in goat
    Before I count from one to five.
    ONE –
    Come on goat show your horn.
    TWO –
    Goat, goat where are you?
    THREE –
    Goat, goat can you not hear me?
    FOUR –
    Goat, goat knock at the door.
    FIVE –

Narrator (*mocking*)
    Once I caught a goat alive.
    It bit my little big toe so
    I had to let that goat go.

Papa Puppeteer (*ignoring him*)
    FIVE –
    Come on down goat,
    Grass to chew

And hills to climb
Horns on the head
And a tail behind.

Narrator
Instead of counting from one to five
Why don't you say once-upon-a-time?
If once-upon-a-time is good enough for a story
It's good enough for a goat.

Once-upon-a-time there was this goat.
A very sensible goat –
In fact he was Lord of the Goats

His horns sat on his head like a crown
And all the high places were his kingdom.

And this goat was so sensible
He was always helping people out of trouble.

One day a hunter named Sushay was returning
    home.
He wanted to give his wife Tasa a surprise.
And out of the earth came an enormous yam.

Papa Puppeteer
Now at a pull of my strings
I bring you a hunter.
And just say the word
And I can bring you a bird,
Instead I bring you a leopard.

Narrator
Come on, Papa Puppeteer,
Don't forget to mention his spear
For what good is a hunter without a spear?

Papa Puppeteer
The same as a house without a roof.

Narrator

Throw a banana into the air
And this hunter
Will peel it with his spear.
This is no lie
Cross my toes and swear to die.

Throw a coin into the air
And this hunter
Will pin it to the ground
Head or tails
At the tip of his spear.

Once a boy's kite was hooked to a tree
The boy began to cry.
The hunter hurled his spear
In a circling throw,
Soon the kite was free
Dancing in the breeze
Climbing on the wind
Mounting to the sky.

There was the speed of
A hawk in his eye
There was the strength
Of a river in his arm
There was a suddeness
Of lightning in his feet.

Papa Puppeteer

See how he moves
In stealthy crawls and creeps,
See how he springs
In nimble bounds and leaps.
And all this he does without the slightest rustle.
Not the faintest echo of a sound.
Soon some animal is brought to ground,

Maybe a lion, a leopard, a deer.
And in its side, a spear.

Narrator

All over the land he was famous for his skill with
  his spear
But he was also known for the kindness in his
  heart.

For while some hunters killed
And killed for fun
Sushay only killed for food.
And he always spoke politely
To the Lord of the Goats
As if he was praying to a god.

Sushay

Master mountain goat
Horned friend of the heights
Send us one of your kind.

We kill only because we are hungry
We hunt no more than necessary.

Master mountain goat
Horned friend of the heights
Send us one of your kind.

Our hand is steady
Our spear is ready.

And there are many mouths to feed.

In our hands a spear
In our hearts a prayer.

Narrator

So now Sushay comes to a river
Where his canoe is waiting.

Papa Puppeteer
But I see no river, no ripple of water.

Narrator
(*stylishly producing long flowing scarf for river*)
Out of my sleeve comes a breeze
And out of a breeze a river.

And Goat wishes to cross this river.

Goat
Hello brother Sushay
Help me cross this river.

Narrator
Says Goat.

Sushay
But you'll eat my yam.

Leopard
But I won't.

Narrator
Says Leopard.

Sushay
But you'll eat my goat.

How can I carry a goat, a leopard and such a
   big yam across the river? My canoe is too
   small.
If I carry leopard first to the other side, then
   I would have to leave goat with yam, and goat
   will surely eat it up.
If I carry yam and leave leopard with goat, then
   leopard will surely eat up goat. What am I to do?
Oh, if only I had a bigger canoe.
How can I carry goat, leopard and yam across
   this river?

It is getting late and I want to surprise Tasa with
  this yam.
At times like today I really wish we had a child.
A son or a daughter would have been a big help
  to keep an eye on this yam so that goat doesn't
  touch it, an extra pair of eyes and hands would
  be so useful.
The moment my back is turned leopard is going
  after goat, and goat is going after yam.
The problem is I can only carry across one at
  a time.
I wonder if I were to put yam on my head and
  lift goat in my lap. Oh that is no good because
  I need my hands free for paddling.
Leopard, you seem to be enjoying my problem.
Well, let me say, you won't get your hands on
  goat, so don't even begin to entertain the idea
  in your head.
Goat, what are you staring at? Have you any
  bright suggestions?

Goat
  You can take me over first.

Sushay
  All right, get in the canoe and sit still. No climbing
  about.
  Remember, this is a river, not a mountain slope.
  Away we go.

Goat
  Down the river in a canoe
  Down the river we float
  One man and a goat.
  Leopard and yam can always wait
  The wind on my horns
  Is feeling so great.

Sushay
So far so good. What happens now?

Goat
You must go and bring yam.

Sushay
But if you think I'll be leaving yam with you,
my bearded friend, you'll have to think again.

Goat
No, after you have brought yam safely across
    the river,
you will have to take me back with you.

Sushay
I thought you were suggesting that I leave yam in
    your company.

Goat
Not at all. But now it will be leopard's turn to
    go across.

Sushay
Alright, Mr Spotted Skin, do as goat suggests,
    and get in that canoe.
You're going for a little trip.
Now don't start any of your springing antics,
    you hear.
And when we get to the other side, I'll be leaving
    yam with you.
At least, you have no interest in eating yam,
I can come back for you, goat.

I knew there was a way to solve the problem.

Goat you are a genius. I won't be long. Wait here
    for me.

Goat

I'll be waiting.

Sushay

And since you have been so helpful, when I
    come back
I'll sing for you a special canoe song as we drift
    along the river.

Down the river in a canoe
Down the river we float
One man and a goat.

I like the way the water flows
Wherever the river goes
There we go, me and you.

Down the river in a canoe
Down the river we float
Oh what a sensible boat
For one man and a goat.

Narrator

Then the Lord of the Goats looked at Sushay
    and said:

Goat

Have no fear.
You are a man of the spear but you have a kind
    heart.
You are not one to complain.
You welcome the sun. You welcome the rain.
You always give thanks for life.
The time has come for me to grant you a wish.
I, Lord of the Goats, will repay your kindness
Simply say what's in your heart.

Sushay

In my heart I always wished for a child.

Nothing would bring me more joy
Than to have a baby girl or boy.

Goat
You have made a wise wish.
Some men might have wished for gold.
But a child is a treasure to hold
And that time will come, Sushay, I promise you
    that time will come.

Papa Puppeteer
You must tell me, did Sushay get his wish?

Narrator
Patience, Papa Puppeteer.
First, Sushay must return home and tell his wife
    Tasa.

Lord of the Goats from his throne on high
Watches his friend Sushay wave goodbye
Watches Sushay on his hunter's feet.

Stepping through the bissi-bissi grass
Stepping over the kissi-kissi stone
Sushay can't wait to get home to tell his wife
    the news.
A child. A child.
The Lord of the Goats has promised us a child.

And as he hurries he sings a song.

Sushay (*singing*)
A child is a treasure to hold.
A child is better than gold.
And Lord of the Goats has promised us a child
And Lord of the Goats has promised us a child.

Narrator
And while Sushay is busy singing

His wife Tasa is going to see
Ni-Ni the wise woman.

Tasa

Time is getting on. Time is getting on.
I have made pots of all kinds,
Pots of all shapes and sizes,
Wide-mouth pots for cooking,
Small-mouth pots for keeping honey,
Long-neck pots for fetching water
But it breaks my heart to grow old
And have no child to cuddle and scold.

Papa Puppeteer

But why should Tasa leave her pot-making
And go to see Ni-Ni the wise woman?
Why should she leave her cooking pots, her
    honey pots, her water pots,
To go and see this wise woman?
And how are you so sure she is really wise?

Narrator

As sure as a needle has an eye
And my bell has a tongue.

As sure as a baby likes to cry
And the moon is round.

As sure as a bird is to sky
As a snake is to ground.

I tell you Papa Puppeteer
Ni-Ni the wise woman
could read the secrets of a circle or a square.

Believe me what you and me would call far

Ni-Ni the wise woman would call near.

Papa Puppeteer
But you still haven't told us
Why Tasa would want to leave her pots
and go to see someone
Who reads the secrets of a circle or a square
and calls far near?

Narrator
Because Tasa wanted to hear
the truth from the mouth of Ni-Ni.

For so long she had prayed for a child
The days had grown into years.
Now Tasa wanted to hear if she and her husband
  Sushay
Would ever be child-lucky.

Would they ever have a little one?
Time was getting on. Time was getting on.

Papa Puppeteer
We are all getting on.
But what happened when she reached the hut
  of Ni-Ni the wise one, the see-far woman?

Narrator
Ni-Ni was already waiting to greet her
and this is what she said –

Ni-Ni
The path that brought you here
told me you were coming.

You will have a child
But take care of its free spirit.

Tasa
I'll do as you say
For Ni-Ni always speaks wisely.

160

What are the signs
That say I will have a child?

Papa Puppeteer
Yes, what are the signs
That say Tasa will have a child?

Ni-Ni
Stones have their ways of telling us things
and shells have their secrets.

But today we will look for other signs.

See, here is a square.

Narrator
See, here is a square.

Ni-Ni
See, here is a circle.

Narrator
See, here is a circle.

Ni-Ni
Into the square I place a gift of yam.

Narrator
Into the square she has placed a gift of yam.

Ni-Ni
Into the circle I place a gift of corn.

Narrator
Into the circle she has placed a gift of corn.

Ni-Ni
Welcome fowl with wing
Welcome goat with horn
Welcome shadows that listen.

Narrator

See, out of nowhere a goat has appeared.
It passes the yam inside the square.
It is eating the corn inside the circle.

Ni-Ni

Here is the sign before your very eyes.

Tasa

What can it mean?
The goat has gone for the corn and left the yam.

Ni-Ni

Oh life is full of surprises.
Imagine, goat is leaving his favourite yam
And instead is going after the corn.
You will be holding a child before long.

Tasa

Oh Ni-Ni, who always speaks so wisely,
I can't begin to say how much your words
     please me.
I can't wait to tell my husband Sushay.
The voice of a child will bring a new music
     to our days.

Ni-Ni

But Tasa, the signs tell me
This will be a child of special ways.
Take good care of its free spirit.

Tasa

She can help me fetch firewood
And collect honey from the beehives.
What a difference she will make to our lives.

I can also teach her to make pots
Which reminds me, I almost forgot,
Here is a honey-pot I have made for you.

Ni-Ni
Thank you for the pot.

Tasa
And thank you for the good news.
I must hurry home and tell Sushay.

Ni-Ni
But remember take good care of its free spirit.

Tasa (*singing*)
A child can be naughty
A child can be wise
Blessed be the child
like the stars in the skies.

Mama, Mama, Mama, Mama.

A child can bring joy
A child can bring pain
Blessed by the child
like the falling rain.

Mama, Mama, Mama, Mama.

I wish for a child
Of my flesh and bone
But if I found a child
I'd call it my own.

Mama, Mama, Mama, Mama.

*As Tasa sings her song, Sushay walks in the opposite
direction singing his song.*

Papa Puppeteer
While Tasa is making her way home
Her husband Sushay is hurrying home too.

Stepping through the bissi-bissi grass
Stepping over the kissi-kissi stone

He meets up with Kaba
a young woodcarver who is always dreaming
of making the most beautiful drum in the world.

Narrator
But I see no carver.

Papa Puppeteer
Look no farther
Look no harder
Now I bring you Kaba the carver.

Narrator
So what's stopping him from making
the most beautiful drum in the world?

Papa Puppeteer
He still can't make up his mind
from which tree to carve this special drum.
He still can't make up his mind
which animal skin to use for this drum.

Narrator
Kaba was dreaming about this drum as usual
when he heard Sushay call out to him, 'Greetings
    Kaba'.

Kaba
Greetings Sushay, why are you in such a hurry?
And where are you going with that child on
    your head?

Sushay
What child? Can't you see this is a yam?

All that dreaming of making
the world's most beautiful drum
is confusing your brain.
Or are you beginning to imagine things?

Kaba

No, Sushay, I swear it looked to me
as if you were carrying a child on your head.
I have never seen such a gigantic yam.

Sushay

Well, Kaba, you are still very young.
Remember, there are mysteries in the sky and
in the ground.

Kaba

Maybe, Sushay, I can help you fetch your yam.

Sushay

Not today, my good friend. Sushay will fetch
this yam alone.
I had enough problems trying to get it across
the river.
I don't know what I would have done if goat
wasn't around.
There was I with leopard, goat and this giant of
a yam
trying to get to the other side of the river
and I was only able to carry one at a time.

Kaba

No problem at all, brother Sushay.
All you had to do was to take across goat first.
Then take yam. After yam is safe on the other
side
take goat back with you.
Leave goat by himself and take leopard to the
other side.
All you need to do now is return for goat, simple
as that.

Sushay

How did you work that out?

You must have the genius of a goat inside that
    brain.
I thought all that brain contained
was dreams of making the most beautiful drum
    in the world.
By the way, how is that dream-drum coming
    along?

Kaba
Brother Sushay, what can I say?
It is coming along, but coming along in my dream.
I still cannot decide which tree
will be best for the body of the drum.
I still cannot decide which animal's skin
will be best for the top.

Sushay
Well, my friend, I must leave you to dream
    of your drum.
I am in a hurry to take this yam to my wife.
I have been fetching it for a while
And it is beginning to grow heavy.

Kaba
Are you sure you don't want me to help?

Sushay
Thanks for the offer Kaba.
But I have not very far to go
and I wish to surprise my wife.

Kaba
And she may surprise you too.

Narrator
While Sushay is stepping over the bissi-bissi grass
stepping over the kissi-kissi stone.

Just then his wife Tasa is hearing a cry
a gentle scream, a gentle moan.

Tasa

This is no animal I swear,
This is no animal caught in a snare
This is no creature caught in a trap.

I can't believe my eyes. A baby girl.
Who could have left you here all alone?
Oh little one, I must take you home
for you are a blessing that has been sent.
What a surprise my husband will have.

We shall bring you up as our own.
Maybe this is what Ni-Ni the wise woman meant
when she said I'll be holding a child before long.
Oh little one, my joy, my song.
What milk is this in the corners of your mouth?

Papa Puppeteer

But what was a baby doing in the bush,
at a fork in the path
behind a rock beside the track
not far from the white anthill?
And with milk in the corners of its little mouth?

Narrator

Why is north north and south south?
Why is sky blue and grass green?
Why is the wind never seen?
Too many questions will get us nowhere
Don't you agree Papa Puppeteer?

Papa Puppeteer

Very well, but tell me this.
What will Tasa say to her husband
if they were to meet up on the way home?

Narrator
> What can a childless woman say to her husband
> when she has found a baby in the bush
> at a fork in the path
> behind the rock beside the track
> not far from the white anthill?

Papa Puppeteer
> What can a childless husband say to his wife
> when she tells him she has found a baby in the
>   bush
> at a fork in the path
> behind the rock beside the track
> not far from the white anthill?

Narrator
> We will soon find out, Papa Puppeteer,
> for those are Sushay's footsteps coming near.

Sushay
> I have brought goat safely across the river.
> I have brought leopard too without any trouble.
> And of course this wonderful giant yam.
> All thanks to goat.
> Soon I'll be home
> and my wife will get the surprise of her life.
>
> But I hear someone coming.
> It looks like Tasa, unless my eyes are fooling me.
> I wonder what she is carrying so carefully
>   wrapped up
> It must be one of her pots.
> I'll pretend as if I have not seen her,
> so as to surprise her.

Tasa
> And I'll pretend as if I haven't seen him,
> so as to surprise him.

And I'll not show him the baby right away,
I'll wait until he asks what are you carrying
    there?

Sushay
And I'll not show her the yam right away,
I'll wait until she asks what are you carrying
    there?

Papa Puppeteer
Who will be the first to speak?
Sushay carrying the enormous yam
or Tasa carrying the new-found child?

Narrator
Sushay, of course.
He couldn't wait to show Tasa the surprise.

Sushay
Tasa, dear wife, I did not expect to see you here.

Tasa
Sushay, dear husband, I did not expect to see
    you here either.

Sushay
Oh even if the river grows wider
and the mountain grows taller
Sushay and Tasa will always find each other.

Tasa
Before you tell me of the river and the mountain
you must tell me what it is that you are carrying there.

Sushay
I am so glad you have asked.
Dear Tasa, this is a surprise for you
and it has travelled by foot and canoe.
It has sat beside a leopard,

And I have kept it away from a goat.
Out of the earth, specially for you, this wonderful yam.

Tasa

Oh this yam is truly wonderful.
You were lucky to keep it away from goat.

Sushay

I wanted to bring it myself all the way for you.
This is a King yam, fit for a queen.

Tasa

I have a surprise too for you,
and it is fit for a king.

Sushay

Even a king likes a good surprise.
Don't keep me waiting. What are you carrying
    there?

Tasa

I was waiting for you to ask.
This surprise, dear Sushay, did not travel by canoe
like your wonderful yam,
but it is also a gift that has been sent,
a bundle of happiness.
You will never, never guess.

Sushay

I guess it is that new pot you were making.

Tasa

I have already given that pot to Ni-Ni the wise
    woman.
Oh Sushay, this is no pot, though it has a neck
    and a mouth
And looks as sweet as the honey inside a pot.

Sushay

Tasa, this is no time to speak to me in riddles.
Can't you see I am dying to find out?

Tasa

Take a look for yourself. What do you see?

Sushay

A child! A child! I cannot believe my eyes.
Here am I bringing you a yam as a surprise,
and what do you bring for me? A child.
Now I am the one who has been truly surprised.

Tasa

Aren't you going to ask me where I found this
child?

Sushay

Where did you find this child?

Tasa

I was returning from Ni-Ni the wise woman,
she had just told me that before long I will have
a child
then suddenly there in the bush
at a fork in the path
behind a rock beside the track
not far from the white anthill
I found this little treasure wriggling on the ground.

Sushay

Lord of the Goats had promised
that my wish for a child will come true.

Papa Puppeteer

And the time has come.

Tasa
Ni-Ni the wise woman had told me
that before long I will have a child.

Ni-Ni
So said, so done.

Tasa
Oh Sushay, our prayers have been answered.
I feel so happy, my heart is like a harvest.

Sushay
At our age we have been blessed.
This child will receive the rain of our tenderness.

Tasa
Though she is not of our flesh and bone
we will care for her as our very own.

Ni-Ni
Just look at Tasa and Sushay.
Words cannot say how much they are pleased.
Now Tasa has a daughter whose hair she can
     braid with small beads.
A daughter to help her crack mongongo nuts.
A daughter to help her with the making of pots.

Goat
Now Sushay has a daughter to help him follow
     animal tracks.
A daughter to help him sharpen his arrow tips.
A daughter to help with the setting of traps.

Ni-Ni
A daughter to whom they can tell lots of stories.

Goat
For the stories of our ancestors belong to the
     children.
And this child is a very special child.

Tasa
Now we should hurry home with our little one,
and let her rest on a warm goatskin covering.

Sushay
But first let us give her a name.
I can whisper a name into her left ear
and you can whisper into her right.

Tasa
The moment she has begun to sneeze
this is a sign that the name has made her pleased.

*The couple bend over the baby whispering various
names into her ears, until at the sound of Odessa, the
child lets out a sneeze.*

Tasa and **Sushay**
Oh she has sneezed!
The name Odessa has made her pleased.
Yes, Odessa it shall be.

Goat (*now visible to Tasa and Sushay*)
You have named her well,
and I know you will shower her with love and
   care.
But remember the words of the one with the
   horns and beard.
Never, never, must blood be allowed to spill
from the toes of the child on a full-moon night.
Be ever watchful in her sixteenth year.

Tasa and **Sushay**
We will make sure that doesn't happen. Have
   no fear.

Ni-Ni
And remember the words of the one
who speaks through the circle and the square.

You have found a child of special ways.
Look after her free spirit to the end of your days.

Papa Puppeteer
Let the name of Odessa be carried on a breeze,
Let the name of Odessa be known to the trees.

Narrator
Let the name of Odessa be told by my bell
as the voice of the sea is heard in a shell.

Tasa and **Sushay** (*singing together*)
Odessa, she's a treasure, a treasure to hold
Odessa, she's better than silver and gold.
Thank you Lord of the Goats for the gift of this
    child
Thank you Lord of the Goats for the gift of this
    child.

We'll watch over her wherever she goes
We'll follow her to where the river flows
We'll be with her when the full moon glows
No blood will spill from Odessa's toes
No blood will spill from Odessa's toes.

*Tasa and Sushay slowly walk off singing their duet.
Narrator and Papa Puppeteer exit in procession singing
the song. Lord of the Goats is alone on stage.*

Goat
Remember, Sushay, you must take care
That when she is in her sixteenth year
and on a night when the full moon glows
Be sure no blood is spilled from her toes.

Act Two

Towards the end of the interval, the Narrator in costume mingles among the audience, ringing a bell and inviting them to return to their seats for the second half.

Narrator (*off stage*)
  By the power of horn and beard on face
  I beg you, people, return to your place.
  In the name of Odessa as told by my bell
  I promise you there's more of my tale to tell.

  (*on stage*)
  As there are many secrets in the skin of a drum
  Life has many mysteries none can fathom.

  When Odessa was only a toddler
  She was causing Tasa and Sushay great wonder.
  Already she was running over stones
  And making nimble leaps among the rocks.

  By the age of seven Odessa was more than a
    handful.
  In fact she was causing the old couple lots of
    thrills.
  Leaping from rock to rock. Climbing up slopes
  As if she wanted to discover the secret of the hills.

Papa Puppeteer
  It's alright for you, Ringabell,
  To speak of mysteries none can fathom
  But such a child deserves a smack on the bottom.

Narrator

If they were to smack Odessa's bottom
every time she got up to her climbing pranks
they'd be smacking her for most of the day.

Tasa and Sushay have to watch her with a careful
  eye
or, next thing you know, she'd be climbing to
  the sky.
There she goes again. Tasa will have a job finding
  her.

*Tasa tries to find Odessa. Odessa, as a seven-year-old is
up a tree.*

Tasa

Odessa. Odessa. Where is this child?
I told her to play in the shade of this tree.
I have no time for hiding and seeking.
Odessa. Has anybody seen Odessa? Where is she?

*Narrator invites a response from children in the
audience as in pantomime.*

Odessa

I'm here.

Tasa

Here where?

Odessa

Up here.

Tasa

Up here, where?

Odessa

In the tree, Mama.

Tasa

    I thought I said play in the shade of the tree
    I did not say play in the branches.

Odessa

    The branches are more fun than the shade.

Tasa

    What are you pretending to be?

Odessa (*making the sound of a goat*)
    BAAAAAY!

Tasa

    I see. You're pretending to be a goat.
    Well, come on down and let me comb your beard.

Odessa

    Watch me, Mama. I can jump
    from the highest branch to the farthest rock.

Tasa

    If I watch you, my hair will turn grey.
    Leave the highest branch to the birds
    Leave the farthest rock to the mountain goats.
    Come on down, child, enough climbing for
      one day.

Odessa

    Mama, up here among the branches
    I make friends with the wind.

Tasa

    Down here you can make friends with a little
      work.
    Let us go and gather nuts and fresh berries.
    I saw some ripe ones not far away.

Odessa

Up here I can see the bees building their hive.
Look Mama. Their hive is shaped like a pot.

Tasa

Let the bees get on with their business.
If you wish, we can go digging for clay
Then you can help me make a honey pot.
I am waiting for you to come down.

Odessa

Come up and catch me.
It's easy, Mama. Watch me.
One foot so. One foot so. And up you go.

Tasa

If you are deaf to my talking
Then maybe a song will open your ears.

Tasa sings.

Odessa, Odessa, won't you come down,
It's safer to play on the ground.
Odessa, Odessa, come down from that tree.
Odessa, Odessa, please listen to me.

Odessa (*sings in reply*)

Oh Mama, oh Mama, I'm not coming down,
The tree is more fun than the ground.
Up here I am near to the birds and the bees.
Oh Mama, won't you like to sit here beside me?

Tasa

Ah! What can you do with such a child?

Papa Puppeteer

Oh she doesn't surprise me at all.
What can you expect from a child
that has been found in the bush,

at a fork in the path
behind a rock beside the track
Not far from the white anthill?
Do you really expect her to keep still?

Narrator
Too many questions, Papa Puppeteer.
You are the one to pull the strings
I am the one to tell of wondrous things.
If Tasa cannot get her to come down
Then, maybe Sushay, the hunter, will.

Sushay enters.

Tasa
I am so glad that you have come back.
Odessa is up in that tree.

Sushay
There is nothing she likes better than to climb.

Tasa
Now she says, she is not coming down
I tried asking her to come and help me
gather nuts and berries.
I tried asking her to come with me
digging for clay by the river
I even tried singing a song.

Sushay
Have you tried scaring her?

Odessa, if you don't come down from that tree
Leopard will have you for his meat.
Odessa, if you don't came down from that tree
Leopard will nibble your feet.

Odessa
I will come down when leopard loses his spots.

Sushay

Oh this child. The things she says!
Where did you learn that?

Odessa

I learnt it from the wind.

Sushay

The same wind that taught you all that
Will blow you down from that same branch.

Odessa

The wind will have to catch me first.
Look, Papa, how fast I can climb.

Sushay

I know you are a good climber
But I am afraid you will fall and hurt yourself.

Odessa

I can jump from the highest branch
to the farthest rock. I like to feel the stones
under my feet.

Sushay

Since you like to feel the stones under your feet
why not come down? I promise you
Papa will take you to the mountainside.
There you can play with the goats.

Odessa

I have already been to the mountainside
and I have already played with the goats.

Sushay

What are you talking about?

Tasa

That child is a dreamer. If she is not busy climbing
she is busy pretending all sorts of things.

Who knows, you may have better luck than me.
Why don't you sing her a song, she might come
down.

Sushay (*sings*)
Odessa, Odessa, won't you come down,
It's safer to play on the ground.
Odessa, Odessa, come down from that tree.
Odessa, Odessa, please listen to me.

Odessa (*sings in reply*)
Oh Papa, oh Papa, I'm not coming down
The tree is more fun than the ground
Up here I am near to the birds and the bees.
Oh Papa, won't you like to sit here beside me?

Tasa
See, the song is no good. It is not working.

Sushay
If the song will not bring her down, what will?

Tasa
Why don't we ask Ni-Ni, the wise woman, to help?

Ni-Ni enters.

Tasa
Oh Ni-Ni, I have just this moment called your
name.

Ni-Ni
Ni-Ni hears many things
and names as you know have wings.

Sushay
I can tell you something else
that behaves as if it has wings.
And that is a child that climbs a tree
and refuses to come down.

Tasa

    We have tried talking to her.
    We have tried singing to her.
    She still will not come down.
    Ni-Ni, what can you do to help us?

Ni-Ni

    I will do what I will. What goes up must come
       down.
    Odessa, what are you doing up in that tree?
    Are you trying to find out the colour of the wind?

Odessa

    No, I am trying to plant a seed in the sky.

Tasa

    Did you hear that?
    Now the child is giving Ni-Ni back-chat.
    Odessa, remember you are talking to Ni-Ni, the
       wise woman.

Ni-Ni

    Oh, don't worry.
    She is more clever than her years.
    So when you have planted the seed in the sky
    What sort of fruit will it bear?

Odessa

    The moon and the stars.

Ni-Ni

    The child answers wisely.
    But how will you reach to water your tree in
       the sky?

Odessa

    The rain will do that for me.

Ni-Ni
Who taught you these things?

Odessa
The wind that tickles the beard of the goat.

Ni-Ni
Come down and tell me some more.
Your head is young but your ideas are old.

Odessa
I'm not coming down. I said so before.

Ni-Ni
Are you going to sleep in that tree?
Leopard will have you for his meal.

Odessa
I see no leopard.

Ni-Ni
Oh yes, you will.

*Leopard is conjured up beneath the tree – possibly a
shamanic transformation by Ni-Ni.*

Leopard
Little girl, come down from that tree.
I promise I will not eat you.

Odessa
I promise I will come down,
if you can tell me one thing.
How many spots do you have on your skin?

Leopard
Little girl, you know that I do not know how
    to count.

Odessa
Then I won't be coming down until you learn.

Leopard
 After I have learnt to count my spots, will
   you come down?

Odessa
 I will come down after you have lost your spots.

Leopard
 How can a leopard learn to lose his spots?

Odessa
 When you have found the answer
 You will be as wise as a goat with a beard.

Leopard
 I prefer to keep my spots
 than to be as wise as a goat with a beard.

 Leopard disappears. Ni-Ni reappears.

Ni-Ni
 Odessa, you are too clever for Leopard.
 Even Leopard could not make you scared.
 Now Ni-Ni will speak to you
 through the circle and the square.

 In the circle, see, I have placed some nuts
 In the square, see, I have placed a leather pouch.

 If I put the nuts into the leather pouch
 the nuts will be safe.

 Now I wish to hide the leather pouch
 in the rafter of my hut

 but the rafter is too high for me.

 Who will climb up there to hide my leather pouch?

 Will Tasa climb up there for me?

184

Papa Puppeteer

No, Tasa will not climb up there for you.

Ni-Ni

Will Sushay climb up there for me?

Papa Puppeteer

No, Sushay will not climb up there for you.

Ni-Ni

Then who will climb up there for Ni-Ni?
Maybe Odessa will climb up there for me.

Odessa

That is easy.

Ni-Ni

So Odessa will help to hang up the nuts for me?
It will be fun climbing to the top of the hut.
But how will you do so if you remain in that tree?

Odessa

All right then, I will come down.
One foot so. One foot so. And down I go.

Odessa climbs down.

Tasa

I knew Ni-Ni would eventually find a way
of getting you to come down from that tree.

Odessa

Ni-Ni has promised that I can help to hang nuts
from the rafter of her hut.

Tasa

And you can do the same for me
but first we must go and gather the nuts.

Ni-Ni

And I'll go to see if Leopard is counting his spots.

All leave except Sushay. The Lord of the Goats appears to him.

Goat
I see Sushay you are deep in thought.
I can tell by the look on your face.

Sushay
The child seems happiest in high places.

Goat
No harm will come to the child
no matter how high she climbs.
But remember, Sushay, you must take care
That when she is in her sixteenth year
and on a night when the full moon glows
Be sure no blood is spilled from her toes.

Sushay
We will look after her well.

The Lord of the Goats disappears.

Narrator
And surely they looked after her well.
I swear by the sound of my bell.
Odessa grew up a helpful child.

She helped Tasa gather berries and nuts
and make designs on her pots.

She could recognise any animal by its tracks
and help Sushay to set small traps.

By the light of the fire
they told her stories and played games.

And so she grew up.

Time, as they say, moves like a bird in a breeze
and from a child gathering nuts and berries,

and listening at night to bedtime stories,
soon Odessa was a confident sixteen-year-old,
moving with the ease of a river over stones
and the gracefulness of a mountain goat
up and down the grassy slopes.

But they remembered the warning
from the Lord of the Goats.

That in her sixteenth year
they should take extra care
that when the full moon glows
no blood is spilled from Odessa's toes.

One day when Odessa was sixteen years old
who should come to visit Tasa?
None other than Kaba, the carver.

Tasa is seen among her pots.

Kaba
Greetings Tasa.

Tasa
Greetings, stranger. I have not seen you for ages.
What good wind has blown you to my door?

Kaba
Oh Tasa, can you not read my thoughts?

Tasa
I am a maker of pots, not a reader of thoughts.
But I suppose you are still dreaming
of carving the most beautiful drum in the world.

Kaba
I have tried every tree. I have tried every skin.
Yet I can find no sound to my liking.

Tasa

The trouble is you can never make up your mind.
You keep changing like the wind.

Kaba

This time I may have found the answer.

Tasa

How many times have I heard you say that?

Kaba

Something tells me I am getting closer
to the world's most beautiful drum.

Tasa

You still haven't said why you came to see me.

Kaba

Well, the other day I went to see Ni-Ni, the wise
woman.
Can you guess what she told me?

Tasa

First you want me to read your thoughts.
Now, you want me to guess what Ni-Ni told you.
Is this one of your games you are playing?

Kaba

No game, Tasa. I have never been more serious.
Ni-Ni has told me that my dreams may lie in a
pot.

Tasa

What do you mean?

Kaba

For years I have been trying all kinds of wood.
I have carved so many solid logs
my hands feel like the bark of a tree.

Then Ni-Ni says to me, 'Have you thought
of stretching a skin across a simple pot?'

Tasa
So you have come to me for a pot?

Kaba
Now you are reading my thoughts.
As soon as Ni-Ni gave me that advice
I said to myself, who is the best person
To make me such a pot?
Tasa of course. She'll make me a pot
that will be perfect for a drum shell,
and by the time I have stretched the skin
Oh the drum will sing like a bell.

Tasa
I will do all I can to make the right pot
for the drum of your dreams.
But right now I am too busy to show you around.
You can tell my daughter the shape you wish
    for your drum.

Odessa appears. Kaba is speechless in admiration.

Tasa (*to audience*)
The dreaming carver seems to be struck dumb.

Odessa
What is the matter? Have you lost your tongue?

Kaba (*flustered*)
So many pots are throwing me in confusion,
Now I am not sure which shape is best.
A square shape or a round?

Odessa (*ironic*)
What about a bowl shape? A cup shape?
A bottle shape? A goblet shape?

Kaba (*dreamily*)
A pot light enough for me to hold in one hand
and to play with the fingers of the other hand.
Or maybe a pot to be held under the arm
and played with both hands.
Then again a pot can always stand on the ground.

Odessa
Have you not seen one that you like?

Kaba (*to audience*)
How can she ask such a question?
If I were to say I've seen perfection
I would be saying with my tongue
what my heart has already found,
for my heart has become a drum.
If she comes any closer, she will hear it pound.

Odessa (*to audience*)
Mama was right when she whispered to me
that this Kaba is a dreamer.
But dreaming fills his face with a simple beauty
even if all he ever dreams about is a drum.

Kaba
I still can't make up my mind.

Odessa
I can see you think deeply about this drum.

Kaba
All my life, why, do you know much about drums?

Odessa
Not much.
Only that a drum can imitate
the snarl of a leopard
or the cry of a bird.

Only that a drum can be heard
far and wide
and that the drummer must say thanks
to the animal that has given up its hide
and must say sorry to the tree
that has been cut down.

Kaba (*impressed*)
Who taught you such things?

Odessa
The wind that carries the voice of your drum
The same wind tickles the beard of the goat.

Kaba
What else has the wind taught you?

Odessa
You must come with me to the mountains
when the moon is full
and there you will learn many things.

*Tasa overhears the conversation. She becomes
concerned.*

Tasa
What are you two talking about?

Kaba
The wind.

Tasa
Have you come all this way
to discuss the wind with my daughter?
No wonder you can never succeed
in carving that drum of yours.
It is getting late, you must leave now.

Kaba
Believe me, dear Tasa, until today

my dream-drum was only a seed.
Now I can see it growing into a tree.

Tasa
You come here to choose a pot for a drum
and end up talking about the wind, a seed and
     a tree.
If you cannot make up your mind, then you
     must go, please go.

Kaba leaves.

Tasa
Odessa, you are to go nowhere tonight.
Do not talk about going to the mountains.
You must not leave this hut.

*Kaba, ecstatic, obviously in love, singing and dancing
by himself. He does not see Sushay observing him.*

Kaba
Kaba, the carver, is learning.
Oh let me succeed.
The tree that is blooming
began with a seed.

Kaba, what is the reason
for your shining cheek?
Kaba, the carver, is feeling
so weak, Oh so weak.

Sushay (*observing from a distance*)
The most beautiful drum in the world
has finally gone to his head.

Tasa, you will not be surprised when you hear this.
Our friend Kaba has now taken
to dancing by himself under the stars.

Tasa
He came today to look at my pots.
Ni-Ni has advised him to use
a pot for the body of his drum.
I asked Odessa to show him around
And what do you think they end up discussing?
    The wind.

Sushay
So now it is the wind
that is drumming inside his cheeks.

Tasa
But I am worried, Sushay.
Tonight I heard Odessa talking to Kaba
about going into the mountains.

Sushay
She likes to be among the mountain goats.

Tasa
She calls them her horned friends.
It isn't easy to keep an eye on her all day and
    all night.
I always try to stop her wandering off to the
    mountainside.

Sushay
Tonight as I stood watching Kaba do his dance
I saw the full moon beginning to rise.

Tasa
I cannot see what harm can come to her.
But to be safe, I've kept her inside the hut,
where I store my pots. At least for tonight.

Odessa (*sings from inside the hut*)
Full moon over the mountains somewhere
    creeping

What are steep slopes for if not for leaping?
I know tonight I won't be sleeping.

Sushay

Did you hear anything?

Tasa

It is only the whistling of the wind among the pots.
That will surely make her sleep soundly.

Sushay

Or maybe it is the night-bird in the breeze.
Goodnight, dear wife, I cannot believe
how quickly these sixteen years have passed.

Tasa

Odessa has given us much joy. What more can
    we ask?

*Odessa is in the hut among the pots. A full moon looks
down.*

Narrator

Tonight of all nights
the full moon glows bright.
Tasa and Sushay are sleeping soundly.
But inside the hut among the pots
Odessa thinks only of the mountains.

Odessa

I can look after myself. They worry too much.
It's a beautiful full-moon night
and they have locked me in. It isn't right.
What harm can come to me on a night like this?
I'd much rather be on the mountainside than
    in this hut.

Odessa breaks into her melancholic song.

Odessa

Full moon over the mountains somewhere
  creeping
What are steep slopes for if not for leaping?
I know tonight I won't be sleeping.

*Kaba appears outside the hut and listens to Odessa's
singing; they speak without seeing each other.*

Kaba

If you wish you can leap over the slopes of my
  dreams.

Odessa

Is that the voice of the one who dreams of a drum?

Kaba

Yes, it is Kaba who will sing your praises
with this drum of his heart.

Odessa

Your words sound sweet as bells.

Kaba

But how much sweeter for me to see your face.

Odessa

Open the door and I will come out.

Kaba opens the door to let out Odessa.

Kaba

Tonight the moon is a beautiful drum.
Even the stars seem to be dancing.

Odessa

On the mountainside the goats will be dancing
  too.

Kaba

I have never seen them.

Odessa

Then I will race you to the mountains.

Odessa leaps into a remarkable run. Kaba cannot keep up with her.

Kaba

Not so fast. Tell me your name.

Odessa

First you must catch me.

Kaba

Wait for me.

I have never seen such speed.

Her legs do not belong to this world.

She is like the wind on two legs.

I can see her tracks.

But she is nowhere in sight.

I cannot believe my eyes

Upon this full-moon night.

Are these the tracks of a girl

Or the tracks of a goat?

Shush. I hear someone coming.

Sushay and Tasa appear, breathless.

Tasa

Kaba, have you seen Odessa?
We found the hut open and she is not there.

Kaba

She's gone racing to the mountains.

Tasa
And without her leather sandals.

Sushay
Let us follow her tracks.

Kaba
I was racing with her, but she is too fast for me.

Tasa
I can hear a cry of pain, maybe it's an animal.

Sushay
Oh no, it is Odessa,
Her foot may have been caught in one on my traps.

Tasa
Kaba, try to follow her tracks.

Sushay
Why did she not put on her sandals?

Tasa
She was determined to go into the mountains.

Sushay
We did all we could to stop her.

*Kaba reappears, supporting Odessa around the
shoulder. She is limping.*

Tasa and **Sushay**
Oh our treasured child, your toes are bleeding.

Kaba
Those are not the toes of Odessa.

The Lord of the Goats reappears.

Goat
I did warn you that in her sixteenth year
Let no blood be spilled from Odessa's toes.

They are the toes of one who belongs to us.
Soon her hooves will climb over these mountains.
She will return to her friends with horns
and taste again the sweet thrill of grass.

But don't look so sad, Sushay and Tasa.
Because you have treated her with tender loving
    care –

For six months of the year she will return to you
In her human form of Odessa,
and for the other six months she will return to us.
Here she will be happy dancing among her
    friends with horns.

As for you, Kaba, you must return to this very
    spot
where blood has flowed from Odessa's toes.
On this spot you will find a tree.
From this tree carve your drum
which will need no animal skin.
That drum will be the one you have been
    dreaming of.

Kaba

    What good is the most beautiful drum
    if I cannot play it for Odessa?

Odessa

    But you will be playing that drum for me, Kaba.
    You remember you said to me
    that you have never seen the dance of the goats?
    I shall be dancing for you, dear Kaba,
    with the moonlight falling on my horns.

Kaba

    Well then, you must always wear

this necklace of shining beads
so I can recognise you.

Sushay and **Taba**
And we will be coming too
to see the dance of the goats.
You are never too old to shake your feet.

Narrator
What about you, Papa Puppeteer?
Are you too old to shake your feet?

Papa Puppeteer
I too will be on the mountains. Have no fear.

Dance of the goats fills the stage.

Odessa
And for six months of the year
I'll be with you, Mama, helping to make pots.
And I'll be with you, Papa, following the tracks.
And as for you, my dear Kaba,
I'll be teaching you to put speed into those legs
and we'll be together.
And to all of you here, I, Odessa say
that on every full-moon night
my hooves will be sending sparks to the milky way.

LITTLE VICTORIES

Shaun Prendergast

To
John, Mary, Alison, Andrea,
Calum and Annie Rose

Little Victories was first presented at the Queen Elizabeth Hall, London, as a co-production between Trestle Theatre Company and Quicksilver Theatre for Children on 11 January 1994. The cast was as follows:

Tony Damien Shaw
Josie Debi Mastel
Debs Anna Carus-Wilson
Gordon Alan Riley

All other parts played by members of the company.

Directed by Graham Walters and Toby Wilsher *Designed by* Mark Wilsher
Lighting by Leslie Phillip Shaw and Jo Joelson
Music by Sally Cook

Characters

Tony
Josie, his friend
Debs, Tony's mother
Gordon, Debs' boy-friend
(*non-speaking, fully masked*)

Josie's mother (*fully masked*)
Josie's doctor (*fully masked*)
Sumo Baby Josie

Chorus of Dogs (*half-masked*)
Sniffer Dog
Gendarme Dog

The dogs play the following non-speaking roles:
French Waiter
French Policemen

The dogs are half-masked and only speak ad-lib gibberish, unless they are speaking in French, which they do fluently, or singing. TV, film and music references can be updated if desired. Most of the special effects can be performed by the cast.

Act One

A kitchen.
   The stage is in darkness.
   At the back of the auditorium floats a luminous moon.
It moves towards the stage, pursued by an excited pack of
dogs, who clamber through the audience. They try to
reach it by standing on each others' shoulders and
climbing on the back of the seats. When the moon reaches
the centre of the stage, the dogs assume a tableau and
begin to howl. It is a mournful sound, both a lamentation
and a prayer. They begin to scamper about, then notice
the audience for the first time. They react with
low-pitched growls at first, then stalk forward
aggressively. One of the dogs starts scratching itself, then
others. A fight ensues. Two dogs exit and the remaining
dogs sniff each others' backsides. They growl at the
audience once more, then resume their howling at the
moon. We hear a baby crying. The lights snap up on Tony
and Josie. Tony is holding a baby (puppet) in his arms,
with its back to the audience. Josie runs towards the dogs,
scaring them away.

Josie Shoo, go on, get out of it! (*to the audience*) Don't
worry about them . . .

Tony Mangy things, making all that noise, they've woke
the baby up. Go on, shoo. (*mimicking Arnold*
Schwarzenegger) 'Hasta la vista, baby! Get out of it, eat
my shorts!'

   The baby cries.

Josie (*to the baby*) Shh . . .

Tony Not you baby. Them babies.

Josie Shut up and introduce us.

Tony (*to the audience*) Okay, this is baby Josie.

Josie Named after me. I'm his friend.

Tony That's Josie, big Josie, instead of . . .

Josie and Tony (*together*) Little Josie.

Josie Shhh, there's a good girl. She's gorgeous.

Tony And I'm Tony. This is my new baby sister. Well, she's not new, she's been around for a while, she'll be one soon.

Josie Is it a year since?

Tony A year. A whole year.

Josie You'll be a big girl soon, eh? Won't you?

Tony Yes, you'll be a big girl. (*to the audience*) Do you wanna see her, eh? Do you wanna meet her?

Josie (*to the audience*) You won't scare her, will you?

Tony 'Cos you are quite scary to look at – all of you! (*He points to an adult member of the audience.*) 'Specially him. (*He ad libs.*) As long as you promise not to frighten her . . . Promise . . .? All right, this is my little sister.

> *The baby puppet is revealed for the first time. It yawns and looks quizzically at the audience.*

See? This is the audience. Not a pretty sight, are they?

Josie Well introduce yourselves. Everybody whisper your name quietly.

Tony Say hallo, Josie.

The baby burps.

She can't talk yet but she made a little sound.

The baby strains, grimaces and fills her nappy.

Josie And she's made a little smell as well, haven't you, Josie?

Tony Oh no.

The stench is overpowering. Josie mimes being sick into the sink.

Oh dear! With any luck the bottom fairy will come and sprinkle some magic dust. Lots of it.

Josie You always make such a fuss.

Tony She needs changing.

Josie Well, change her.

Tony I can't.

Josie Why not?

Tony I'm only eight. I'll have to get Mum to do it.

Josie Why not get Gordon to do it? He's her dad.

Tony Yeah, great idea. We'll get Gordon to do it. Where is he?

Josie He's mending the sink.

Josie reveals Gordon, who is under the kitchen sink attempting to unblock it. The audience cannot see his face.

Tony Gordon! Hey Gordon! (*He kicks Gordon's feet to attract his attention.*)

There is a loud crash as Gordon bumps his head.
Gordon appears. He is a full mask character, a
well-meaning man with a heart of gold, but
uncoordinated. He is rather harassed at the moment.
Josie exits.

She needs changing. Red alert, red alert, thunder bums are
go! Gordon! She has done her dirty, now you must do
your duty. Five, four, three, two, one! Lift off!

Tony hands Gordon nappy changing items; talc, cream,
etc. He throws a clean nappy and it lands on Gordon's
head. Gordon looks unimpressed.

Come on, she's your daughter.

Tony's mum, Deborah Mason, enters. It's raining
outside, her mac is soaking and she looks tired and
bedraggled. She is carrying eight carrier bags stuffed
with food and disposable nappies.

Debs (*snapping*) Tony! Did you wake the baby?

Tony No, she needs changing.

Debs Well don't just stand there, Gordon, get on with it.
I've got to put the shopping away. (*She begins to put the*
shopping away into the kitchen cupboards.)

Gordon sighs heavily and accepts his responsibilities.
He takes the baby from Tony.

Wash your hands before you change her, mind.

Tony No, don't wash your hands!

Debs Stop mucking about, Tony, he's covered in grease.

Tony (*winding Gordon up*) Don't do it Gordon, it's very
dangerous, please!

Gordon is puzzled and alarmed.

Debs Why not?

Tony He's undone the sink. If he tries to wash his hands by pouring water from the taps it'll go down the plughole but the plughole isn't connected to the downward pipe so it'll go all over the floor and the floor will be really slippy and you'll be walking along carrying a big rubbish bag of smelly dirty nappies and you'll slip on the floor and fall and break your neck and you'll be dead and the police will come and they'll arrest Gordon and put him in jail –

Gordon doesn't like the sound of this.

– in a big castle with a mask over his face like Hannibal the Cannibal – 'A plate of fava beans and a nice bottle of Chianti' – and you'll be dead and he'll be in jail and there'll be no one left to look after me and Josie and the council will come and take Josie into care and it'll be just like Charles Dickens, 'Can I have some more sir', 'No you cannot have some more', instead you'll be sold to an evil man with warts on his nose like a bunch of grapes, but then Toxic Avenger will come and put slime all over the man with the warty nose, slobber slobber slobber slobber and Josie will be saved –

Gordon, caught up in the story, goes to defend baby Josie.

– and she'll be adopted by a rich couple who'll live in a huge mansion next to a great beach like *Baywatch*, all wiggle wiggle wiggle 'Help I'm drowning,' 'Cute buns missy,' and the rich people will be really nasty just like in the soaps, and they'll bring Josie up to be really snotty-nosed and I'll be thrown out of the house on to the streets where I'll end up living in a cardboard box and begging, 'Got any spare change please,' and then I'll start taking drugs and I'll end up dead in the gutter and it'll all be Gordon's fault!

Gordon is horrified at this idea.

Debs Well he better go and wash his hands upstairs then, hadn't he?

Gordon agrees with this and hurries off with the baby. Debs also exits.

Tony (*to the audience*) Good old Gordon, gormless Gordon, I love winding him up. See, ever since my dad died my mum's had loads of different boyfriends. Like once, right, this bloke at the squash club took her out, he was called Kevin. And he had a huge nose and a really silly voice. He talked like this, 'Hallo, little man, my name's Kevin.' But he didn't last very long 'cos Mum said he had really bad breath, which is true, right. Steeeeench!

Then the next one was called Matthew, and he was really funny because he was one of those grown-ups who was really old but pretends to be really young. You know what I mean? Like he'd say things like 'Wicked' and 'Bad', and you know fine well they haven't got a clue what they're talking about. So Matthew got the push and then she didn't see anybody for a while, and there was just me and her and it was great, this all happened about a year ago right? And then one day I came in from school . . .

Debs enters in her dressing-gown; she's just washed her hair and put her make-up on.
Tony listens to a Walkman.

Debs Tony, Auntie Lucy is coming round tonight . . . Tony, are you listening to me? (*She switches the Walkman off.*)

Tony I've gone deaf. (*He takes the Walkman off and shouts.*) I've gone deaf!

Debs (*loudly*) No you haven't!

Tony Stop being silly, Mum. Wassamatter?

Debs Aunty Lucy will be looking after you tonight.

Tony Why?

Debs I'm going out. She'll be here soon.

Tony Why are you wearing lipstick?

Debs Now I want you to behave for Auntie Lucy, you can watch telly and she's going to cook you your favourite pizza.

Tony I don't want pizza.

Debs Don't be silly, you love pizza.

Tony Has it got onions in?

Debs I'll have to hurry, he'll be here in a minute.

Tony 'Cos I don't like onions.

Debs But I'll be back by nine o'clock.

Tony I'm not eating it if it's got onions in.

Debs Yes, all right, I'll make sure she takes all the onions out.

Tony Who's he?

Debs After you've had your tea you can watch TV till eight and then it's bedtime, Okay?

Tony Who's he? Who's this He you're waiting for?

Debs Just a bloke.

Tony What's his name? (*to the audience*) She hates telling me their names, she always mumbles this bit.

Debs (*mumbling*) Gordon.

Tony Sorry, what was that?

Debs Gordon.

Tony Just a little bit louder if you don't mind?

Debs Gordon.

Tony Gordon? (*to the audience*) As soon as I heard that name I knew he'd be a plonker. I could sense it. And I was right. Even the dogs at the bottom of our street knew he was a plonker.

> *There is the sound of barking off-stage. Gordon is chased on by one of the dogs we saw earlier. He is wearing a duffel coat over his shell-suit and sandals with socks under them. He carries a present.*

Debs (*to the dog*) SHOO! SHOO! Get out! Go home!

> *Gordon starts to leave.*

Not you, Gordon. (*to the dog*) Shoo!

> *The dog exits.*

Tony. This is Gordon.

Tony Is this your new boyfriend?

Debs Well, we're going out together.

Tony I don't believe it! A duffel coat!

> *Gordon is dismayed by Tony's sarcasm.*

Debs You don't believe what?

Tony You're going out with him?

Debs What's wrong with him?

Tony He looks a total prat.

Debs Says who?

Tony Says me.

Gordon is in the middle, like a tennis umpire.

Debs Yeah?

Tony Yeah!

Debs Is that right?

Tony That's right!

Debs Well luckily you're not going out with him.

Tony Yeah, lucky for me.

Gordon tries to sneak off but Debs hauls him back by the hood of his duffel coat.

Debs Yeah, lucky for me too!

Tony I wouldn't be seen dead with him.

Debs (*whispering*) He's got a present for you.

Tony A present! (*He suddenly smiles and becomes effusive. He mimics Cilla Black.*) 'Gordon, hallo chuck, welcome to *Blind Date*, isn't he lovely, we're going to have a lorra lorra laughs, that's right love, sit down, take the weight off your present.' (*He provides Gordon with a chair.*)

Gordon sits down for a few seconds then gets up and wanders nervously around the kitchen. Everything he touches he breaks; handles come off cupboards, etc.

Debs Good lad. I'm just going to get changed.

Tony Oh no! What are you gonna wear?

Debs None of your business.

Tony Yes it is!

Debs exits. Josie enters from an obscure part of the set.

(*calling after Debs*) You might be walking down the street in some of your stupid clothes and my friends might see you!

Josie You haven't got any friends except me.

Tony Shut up you, I didn't even know you when all this happened.

Josie Your mum looks great.

Tony She looks terrible, she keeps wearing those skin-tight leggings and she's too old for them, I mean let's face it, she's twenty-six, she's ancient, she'll be getting her pension soon.

Josie Well, how do you want her to dress?

Tony She should dress properly, like an old person. Isn't that right, Gordon?

Gordon is fiddling with the kitchen window blind. At the mention of his name he gets a shock and lets go, causing the blind to furl with a clatter. During the following, he picks up the Walkman and begins listening to it.

Josie What, with a hat that ties under her chin –

Tony – and sensible brown shoes –

Josie – and a big tweed coat smelling of ointment –

Tony – she could have one of them baskets on wheels – (*mimicking*) 'My grandchildren are in New Zealand you know . . .'

*Josie and Tony sneak up to Gordon and turn the
Walkman off. Gordon, thinking he's gone deaf, takes
off the earphones and hits himelf on the side of the
head. Tony and Josie mime talking. Gordon gets really
worried.*

(*loudly*) Right, where's this present then, Gordon?

*Gordon is shocked by Tony's loud voice. Tony snatches
the present from Gordon's hands and looks at it
disdainfully.*

What a mess.

Josie It looks very nice. If I'd known you were like this
when I met you I'd never have hid under that table in
France.

Tony Well honestly, it's bound to be rubbish! I mean a
bloke in a duffel coat and sandals isn't going to give you a
Nintendo, is he? This is going to be a smelly present I'll
bet. Something like . . . it's gonna be the *Ladybird Guide
to Playing the Clarinet*. Or socks even. Yeah, he's the sort
of bloke who thinks he can get on your good side with a
box of Maltesers and a pair of socks.

Josie Well unwrap it, then.

*Tony unwraps the present. Light glows from it. There
is thunder and lightning: intimations of the
Death-Dealer world. Josie looks about in wonder.
Tony's eyes remain fixed upon the present.*

Tony, it's gone cold.

Tony It's . . .

Josie There are shadows. I'm scared.

Bits of the room begin to transform into the

*Death-Dealer landscape. Images of a monstrous baby
Josie appear and disappear from mundane places such
as the microwave and the washing machine.*

I'm so cold. There's a cloud across the sky.

Tony (*still transfixed*) It's . . .

Josie Look at Gordon!

*The alphabetical fridge magnets move of their own
accord to spell out 'LIFE AND DEATH', and Gordon
transforms into the Silent Wizard, who is part of the
Death-Dealer game.*

What's happening? What is it?

Tony It's a DEATH-DEALER!

Josie Oh, is that all.

The kitchen, and Gordon, return to normal.

Tony Wow! Death-Dealer, level one hundred.

Josie You dossy thing.

Tony Mega-wicked, this is the best one yet.

Josie You spawny rat.

Tony State of the art up to the minute grade one top level
stuff.

Josie Well, say thank you to Gordon.

Tony Who'd have thought that a prat like him would get
me a Death-Dealer! And if he buys me this on the first
date what's he gonna buy me when she kisses him for the
first time? I mean, he'll have to give me a car or
something.

Josie He's waiting.

Tony And the first time he sleeps over? He'll have to buy me a house.

Josie You don't deserve friends, you! Serve you right if he doesn't give you the other present!

Tony Another present? He must be rich! Perhaps he's one of them concentric millionaires, what have got lots of money and don't know what to do with it – (*to Gordon*) give it to me, give it to me, you are hypnotized, give it to me concentric millionaire, 'cos they dress like tramps. It's true.

Gordon, hypnotized, falls to his knees.

Right, where's this other present?

Gordon searches on the ground.

Come on, come on, I haven't got all day. What is it, a telly? A computer, a compact disc player, a cuddly toy? What's on the board, Miss Ford?

Gordon finds an envelope and hands it to Tony sheepishly.

Our survey says . . . uhn-uhn! An envelope?

Debs enters dressed in a very glamorous frock. She looks like a million dollars. Gordon wakes from hypnosis only to fall into another trance at the sight of her.

Debs (*noticing the envelope*) Well, open it.

Tony This had better be money!

Debs Tony!

Tony (*to Gordon*) Are you listening, gormless? 'Cos if this is a book token you can stick it up your duffel coat.

Debs Go on, open it.

Tony This is like the Oscars. And the winner is . . . (*He opens the envelope.*) Three tickets to Boe Lounge. Boe Lounge? What's a Boe Lounge?

Debs It's Boulogne. It's in France. Gordon's treating us to a little holiday in France.

Tony I don't wanna go to France. I want a compact disc player.

Debs It'll be nice. We'll get to go on a catamaran.

Tony A catamawhat?

Debs A big catamaran, a Supercat.

Tony Across the sea on a Supercat? What do we do, all hang on to its collar? Is there like a huge tin of Whiskas in France and we hang on and the cat goes meeaaaiiiowww?

Debs It'll be educational.

Tony I don't wanna be educated. I get enough of that at school.

Debs It cost a lot of money.

Tony Well good, he can take the tickets back and buy me a compact disc player instead. And anyway, what's he doing forking out for a trip to France on the first date? It is the first date, isn't it? You can't fool Inspector Morse! Lewis!

Josie Whyaye, sir?

Tony I've got a job for you.

Josie Eeh, I was hoping to get home early, sir, it's the wife's aerobics class.

Tony No such luck, Lewis, now, give me nine pints of beer and a recording of the Brandenburg Concerto. When you've done that, arrest these two for seeing each other in stubterfuge. I mean in subterfudge. Seeing each other in slobterfidge. Have you two been seeing each other behind my back?

Debs I think I heard the doorbell, that must be Aunt Lucy. We'll have to go, Gordon, we're late.

She exits.
Tony circles Gordon like a jackal stalking an injured bird. Gordon looks distinctly uncomfortable.

Tony You've been sneaking around haven't you, seeing my mother on the sly? Lying! Admit it! A typical grown-up trick! You're blushing! I knew it! Guilty!

Gordon is horrified.
The set transforms into a courtroom. Household objects rise and form a dock around Gordon. Josie becomes the judge.

Josie What is the charge?

Tony M'lady, that this man is a hardened criminal who thinks nothing of trifling with the affections of a young widow and attempting to ingratiate himself with her loving son by common or garden bribery. Has he uttered one word in his defence?

Gordon looks speechless.

No! Has he said one word by way of explanation? No! I put it to you that the evidence he has given before this court is nothing more than a tissue of evasion and half truth. A web of deceit and slibbterfadge! In short, Rodney you plonker, a lorry-load of porkies. (*He points off dramatically.*)

A dog appears dressed as a policeman.
Gordon is petrified.

Josie Gordon Stanley Duffelcoat Sandalshoe Walker, you have been found guilty of being a lying grown-up. Do you admit the offence?

Gordon nods pitifully.

It is my painful duty to pass sentence.

Gordon drops to his knees and begs for mercy. The sniggering dog drags him upright again.

You will be taken from this court to the seaside and placed upon a Supercat which will then take off for a very bumpy ride across the water and you'll be joggled around until you're sick and you vomit everywhere . . .

There is the sound of seagulls. The set transforms into a Supercat. Gordon looks queasy. A dog steps forward and commences (in mime) a safety drill demonstration. This includes swimming, screaming, and drowning.

Tony (*to the audience*) Have you ever been on a Supercat? I mean, they're massive.

Josie Hundreds of seats in rows and all these people . . .

Tony And it can be really rough when the wind gets going, and the stewardesses point out all this stuff you have to do in case it sinks.

Josie Seems a bit daft to me.

Tony Why?

Josie I mean, you'll still be in the middle of the sea.

Tony So?

Josie You'd still drown, you'd just die standing up, at least if you stayed on board you could die sitting down.

Tony You're weird.

Josie And you're smelly.

Tony Anyway you're not even supposed to be in this part of the story. I haven't even met you yet.

Josie Right, I'm going. (*to the audience*) Boys are so silly.

Tony (*to the audience*) Girls are so simple. Simple pimple. Pimple!

Josie Suffer.

Josie exits. Debs enters with a couple of drinks from the bar. Everyone sways with the motion of the crossing.

Debs What are you saying about girls, Tony?

Tony Nothing, Mum.

Debs (*handing him a drink*) There's yours.

Tony Thanks. Can I go on deck?

Debs It's too windy, you might get blown away.

Tony You still feeling queasy, Gordon?

Gordon nods.

You've gone green. Don't worry, it'll only last another half an hour, then you can be in France and have lots of lovely French food, like snails and garlic.

Gordon throws up.

Way to go, Gordon. At this rate we'll soon have a bag each. (*He hands sickbags to members of the audience; addressing them.*) Here. Present for you. Don't worry,

you'll all get one. Has anybody got a hat we can borrow?
Or a duffel bag?

Gordon throws up again.

You'd better get used to it folks! I mean we haven't had
carrots since last Tuesday. There's still four and a half
days of dinner to come up yet!

Gordon staggers to his feet.

Debs (*to Gordon*) Toilet?

Tony Oh dear, it's gonna be coming out of both ends, is
it?

Debs (*to Gordon*) Go on, love.

Tony Think about those sprouts we had on Sunday.

Debs I'll be with you in a minute.

Gordon exits.

Tony So I'll just sit here on my own then?

Debs Don't go on love, please.

Tony (*to the audience*) Typical grown-up. When you
want to watch the telly or play games, they tell you to put
them away and talk like a proper person. But when you
want to talk they say . . .

Debs Just sit there and play quietly.

She exits.

Tony I didn't mind. With Death-Dealer you've got to
really concentrate. I mean it's not chucking bricks like
Super Mario, loading up some daft lorry, and it's not just
kung fu kicks and machine guns like some John Claude
Van Dumb film, it's complicated stuff. It's more

complicated than maths! More complicated than
chemicals or hydrology, I'll bet! Before you know it the
game's over and you've arrived at the end. And before we
knew it, we had!

> *The set transforms into France. There are two basic*
> *sets now: a hotel room with a balcony looking out to*
> *the moon, and a café with a fruit stall next to it.*
> *Gordon is in bed in the hotel room.*

France! You ever been there? Anybody ever been to
France? I haven't. I know I pretended that I didn't wanna
come but that was just to get up Gordon's nose. Really it's
a bit of an adventure, I don't know what to expect! Could
be totally flat with no trees and no hills . . . No, there's a
hill, there's a tree . . . Could be bright green with yellow
rivers. No, bricks are red, roads are black . . .

> *A waiter enters and begins setting up a café table. He is*
> *a French half-mask dog. All the French dogs speak*
> *perfect French.*

Perhaps it all looks okay on the surface but underneath it
all the people are turning into onions . . .
deedoodeedoodeedoo, the Twilight Zone. (*He imitates*
Captain Kirk.) 'Oh, Spock, what, are, we, doing, here, in,
this, God-forsaken, land . . . it's so . . . boring . . . there's
loads of people, shopping, driving, riding their bikes . . .
with their little onion legs . . .'

> *The waiter takes offence.*

Nothing personal . . . As it happens it looks like anywhere
else, shops, cafés, boats, but all the names are different!
Boulangerie, pâtisserie . . . wow, those cakes look
fantastic! Gordon would like those, he's very fond of
cream cakes. How ya doing, Gordon?

Gordon sits up in bed, waves feebly and goes back to sleep.

He's still a bit queasy. He's crashed out on the bed, ha ha, and that means me and Mum can go out together.

Debs enters.

Debs Tony, let's get something to eat!

Tony Great, food! Feed me! Feed me!

The waiter hands Tony and Debs a menu. They each take a seat at the café table.

Debs What do you fancy?

Tony What've they got?

Debs (*speaking fluent French*) *Boeuf Bourguignon, huîtres*, a selection of *fromages* –

Tony What's all that?

Debs French food.

Tony I don't want that muck! Why can't we have proper British food? Spaghetti? Or hamburgers? Or pizza or spring rolls or poppadoms?

Debs Well at least try something.

Tony Egg and chips.

Debs *Oeuf pommes frites s'il vous plaît, garçon.*

The waiter writes down the order.

Tony Oy, mate, forget the erffing pom freets, just stick to the egg and chips.

The waiter exits.

(*standing up and shouting*) Gordon? Fancy a fried egg?

You know, a half-cooked one where the white of it's still a bit snotty? A lovely runny snotty egg? We could throw it up to you? And you could throw it up to us? Wimp! Wussy wimp!

Debs Leave him alone, he's still not well.

Tony How long have you known him then?

Debs About a year.

Tony A year! Why didn't you ever bring him home until now?

Debs You know why.

Tony What's that supposed to mean?

Debs You've never liked any of my boyfriends. You've always made it difficult for them.

Tony I haven't.

Debs You have, ever since . . .

Tony Look at the shape of that man's hat!

Debs You know what I'm talking about. Ever since . . .

Tony That car's a funny colour.

The waiter enters.

Oh great, food. I love French food, I'm starving.

The waiter serves them their food, then exits.

Egg and chips. Oh great.

Debs Darling, I'm trying to tell you something very important and you keep changing the subject.

Tony And that's when I saw Josie for the first time ever, right, Mum! Look at that kid!

225

Debs Tony.

Tony This amazing weird kid.

Debs We brought you here for a reason, we thought –

Tony No, I mean it. This incredible-looking kid.

Debs We thought it would be easier for you if we broke the news away from home because the thing about travel is that you get used to the idea of things being different, of things being changed. And nothing can stay the same, you know. Things change. Things live, and grow and die.

Tony But, Mum, Mum, look at the kid.

Debs Tony, I'm going to have a baby, a little brother or sister. And Gordon and me are going to get married when we get back to England. We think we'd like to.

Josie enters. She is pale, bald and heavily wrapped up.

Tony Weird looking! Must be French, maybe all French people look like that, maybe all the rest have been tourists and she's the first French person we've seen. (*to Debs*) Have a baby?

Josie Who are you staring at?

Debs That's right.

Josie You staring at me?

Tony You and Gordon?

Josie You stare at me and I'll punch your teeth in.

Josie's mother (masked) appears, sees her runaway daughter and embraces her.
   Tony is fascinated and stares as Josie's mother attempts to make Josie wear a large woollen cap to hide her baldness. Debs smacks Tony's hand lightly and

226

whispers to him under her breath, trying to get him to stop looking, but he is engrossed.

Josie glowers at Tony, throws the cap to the floor and runs away. Her mother picks up the cap and runs after her.

Debs That's right. Me and Gordon are going to –

Tony I heard. I wasn't trying to change the subject. It's like every time you want to talk about Dad dying, then you tell me I'm trying to change the subject.

Debs You always do try and change the subject.

Tony I wasn't trying to change the subject, I was just looking at the kid.

Debs I saw her.

Tony Weird looking. French.

Debs She isn't French, she's English.

Tony Funny voice.

Debs She's from the North.

Tony She's bald.

Debs She's ill. She's sick.

Tony Probably the food. These chips are disgusting!

Debs I wanted you to hear it from both of us, but I need to know what you think.

Tony I think I'm going to throw up.

Debs I think Gordon will make a very good father.

Tony You're making me sick. He makes me sick. I'm gonna be sick.

Debs We have to talk.

Tony I don't wanna talk. I don't wanna talk to anybody. I hate this place, I hate you and I hate your baby! (*He runs off.*)

Debs (*calling*) Tony –

The waiter enters.

Oh, *pardonnez-moi monsieur* . . . (*She clears the table with an embarrassed fluster and throws money at the waiter. Calling*) Tony, please.

Debs and the waiter exit.
The stage once again takes on a nightmarish quality. A surreal washing-line appears.
Tony enters and hides behind the washing-line. Josie enters and hides at the other end. They don't see each other.

Tony I ran and I ran and I heard her calling me and shouting for the police but it didn't matter, there was no way I was going back to her.

Debs appears.

Debs (*shouting*) Tony, where are you? I'm sorry, I love you, come back . . . Come back love, please. Help! . . . *Au secours* . . . Police . . . *Gendarme* Police? (*with a French accent*) Poleez?

She sees Josie, who wraps a sheet around her head to hide her baldness and pretends to be an old woman.

Où la?

Josie La?

Debs *Où la?*

Josie La?

Debs *Où la la?* Damn . . .

Debs runs off.

Josie (*confronting Tony*) You!

Tony You!

Josie Come looking for a fight?

Tony Any time.

Josie Any time. But not just now.

Tony 'Cos I'm hiding.

Josie 'Cos I'm running away.

Josie exits and the washing-line disappears. Tony hides under the table.

Tony Suddenly the funny kid was gone and I couldn't see Mum and there was nobody, just France, just empty France. She's too old to have a baby. She can't even look after me, letting me run away and get lost and it's cold and it's starting to rain.

A forest of umbrellas appears.

Leaving me alone to make my own way through French umbrellas . . . 'Scuse me, 'Scuse me! She's a terrible mother!

Debs runs on, flushed, panicking.

Debs (*calling*) Tony, Tony! Where the hell are you? I'll strangle you when I get hold of you. (*She exits.*)

Tony You're a terrible mother! Babies, I hate them! What does she want to have a baby for?

*He runs around the stage. Wherever he goes he is
thwarted by images of the monstrous baby Josie; they
pop out of flower pots, emerge from drainpipes, the
cooker, etc. Tony attempts to force them back into their
hidey holes.*

Babies are horrible! A lot of my mates' mums and dads
have had babies and they're really sneaky about it, what
they say is, 'It's going to be really good fun and you'll
really love your little brother or sister,' but what they
mean is some fat bald monster is going to come into your
house, take over the spare room, cover the floor with their
toys, get all the attention and actually take over your life,
actually! Attack!

*A huge sumo wrestler-type baby Josie appears. Tony
squares up to it with the full ritual of sprinkling salt,
etc. Tony and the Sumo Baby wrestle.
Josie enters, running away from her mother. The
Sumo Baby bounces against Tony, who in turn collides
with Josie.
The baby exits.*

Josie Hide! Quick!

Tony Who you running away from?

Josie My mum.

Tony Me too.

*They hide.
Debs enters and frantically runs from one side of the
stage to the other.*

Debs (*calling*) Tony, please, for God's sake, Tony ...

*She exits.
Josie takes a piece of paper from her pocket and*

begins to fold it.

Josie Got a pen?

Tony Yeah. What you making?

Josie A chancer. (*She constructs it.*) See, you fold it like this, then like this, then like this, right? So you have to write instructions on this bit, or fortune-telling things or whatever, and then colours here and numbers there.

Tony What are you making it for?

Josie Helps pass the time when you're hiding. You scared?

Tony No!

Josie I bet you are. I bet it's the first time you've run away. How old are you?

Tony Eight. Nearly.

Josie How old really?

Tony Seven and a bit. How old are you?

Josie Nine. You are scared aren't you? (*She finishes making the chancer.*)

Tony I'm not. Can I have a go?

Josie All right, what's your name?

Tony Tony.

Josie (*with the chancer*) T.O.N.Y. Now choose a colour.

Tony Purple.

Josie P.U.R.P.L.E. Right, now you've got to promise that whatever this says you'll do it.

Tony Promise.

Josie Or you'll die a horrible, painful, lingering death.

Tony Promise.

Josie Cross your heart.

Tony Cross my heart.

Josie Spit on your mother's life.

Tony Spit on me mother's life.

Josie Choose a number.

Tony Six.

Josie (*opening the chancer and reading*) It says 'You must give Josie a kiss.'

Tony What? No!

Josie Shhh.

Tony I'm not kissing you! Try another one.

Josie Well, if you won't do this one than you really will die in agony. We'll use your full name this time. What is it?

Tony Tony Mason. Yellow. Number three.

Josie (*reading the chancer*) 'Take down your trousers and show us your bum.'

Tony No way!

Josie Come on, you've gotta do one of them.

Tony Well I'm definitely not showing you me bum!

Josie Well you'll have to kiss me then.

Tony Oh no. Oh this is horrible . . . I wish I'd never heard of this stupid game.

Josie I'm waiting.

Tony Do I have to?

Josie Yes, after three. One. Two. Three.

She puckers up. He attempts to kiss her briefly but she grabs him by the neck and snogs him. He breaks free, mortified.

Tony (*loudly*) Yeeeeeuuuuurrrrrrrggggggghhhhhh!

Josie Do you want another go?

Tony No I don't!

Josie Shhh. Somebody's coming.

Josie's mother and a Gendarme Dog enter, cross the stage and exit.
    Josie and Tony hide.

Tony Who's that?

Josie My mum.

Tony Who's that with her?

Josie *Gendarme.* French cop.

Tony Thought it might be your dad.

Josie No, my dad's back at the hotel. He had oysters last night. Been throwing up since three this morning. Projectile vomiting, real hughie.

Tony Yeah, Gordon did that last night. Red wine all over white walls. Looked like the revenge of Freddy Krueger.

Josie Well, little bit of sick never hurt anybody. Gordon your dad?

Tony No, he's my mum's boyfriend.

Gordon appears with a Gendarme. They rush across the stage and disappear in the wings, only to rush back again, seconds later. They exit during the following.

That's him, gormless Gordon with the French copper. The John dim, or John don, or Jim Beam or whatever.

Josie *Gendarme.*

Tony You speak French then, do you?

Josie *Mais oui.*

Tony I said do you speak French then, do you?

Josie *Mais oui* means yes.

Tony Oh, I didn't know. Why did you run away from your mum?

Josie I get sick of people staring at me like you did but when I say I'll smash them up Mum gets really worried, then she starts to cry.

Tony Why?

Josie 'Cos she's a mum.

A Gendarme Dog appears.

Tony They've got the dogs on us now.

Josie They'll find us before long. They always do.

A Sniffer Dog enters.
The Sniffer Dog spots Tony and Josie, and points them out to the Gendarme Dog but the Gendarme Dog doesn't notice.

Sniffer Dog (*to the Gendarme dog*) Ici! (*Here!*)

Gendarme Dog (*on its own trail*) Non, ici ici, Michel, ici, ici . . .

Sniffer Dog NON, HENRI, ICI!

Gendarme Dog Ici, here. Ici!

The Gendarme Dog exits.

Sniffer Dog Oh, sacré bleu . . . Qu'est-que c'est le point? Henri est merde . . .

The Sniffer Dog disconsolately follows the Gendarme Dog off.

Tony So come on, tell me, why do you keep running away?

Josie It keeps them on their toes. I ran away at Euro-Disney. Dad got furious and ended up having a fight with Mickey Mouse. Oh Pluto. Oh Minnie, oh goddammm . . .

Tony Euro-Disney? Your mum and dad must be rich.

Josie No. We just travel round so much now there's no time for him to do his job. Where do you live?

Tony London.

Josie I'm coming there in two weeks' time.

Tony Come and see me.

Josie I don't know where you live.

Tony I'll write it down.

Josie gives him the scrap of paper used to make the square for the chancer.

Josie (*referring to the chancer*) You sure you don't want another go?

Tony No I don't. Here, if you're bored, you can play with this. (*He hands her his Death-Dealer.*)

Josie Death-Dealer level one hundred.

Tony Yeah, brand new, just out. I might be the first person in London to have one. First in England.

Josie I got mine three months ago.

Tony Three months? Was it your birthday?

Josie No. I just saw it in a shop and said I liked it and Dad bought it for me. Ever since I've had cancer they've given me everything I wanted.

Tony Colour telly?

Josie Yep.

Tony Portable compact disc player?

Josie Uh-huh.

Tony Good Swatch?

Josie (*showing it to him*) The best.

Tony Ha, I wish I had cancer.

Josie They thought I'd beaten it but I've got another tumour.

Tony Is that one of them things they play in the orchestra?

Josie No that's a tuba. This is a tumour.

Tony Can I have a look? Is it like a big pussy boil? Has it got a scab on it? When nobody's looking in the middle of the night do you pick the scab off and eat it?

Josie No, it's inside.

Tony Inside? That's no fun.

Josie No, it isn't. How far have you got?

236

Tony Level thirty-seven. It's a tough one this one, isn't it?

Josie My doctor keeps telling me she's got to level sixty but I don't believe her.

Tony Your doctor plays Death-Dealer? Good doctor.

Josie She reckons that when you start off it seems impossible but you just have to do little victories, take things in stages, one step at a time. Right, I'm gonna go back to my hotel, they'll have worried enough by now. Thanks for the address.

They emerge from their hiding place.
Josie's mother enters from one side of the stage and Gordon enters from the other. They see their respective children and rush forward to embrace them. Josie's mother takes Josie off-stage.
Tony steps out of Gordon's embrace.

Tony (*addressing the audience*) When Gordon found me I half expected him to try and clip me round the ear but he didn't. He just looked sad and hurt. He wasn't even angry. But Mum was!

They return to the hotel room. Debs is in a furious temper and throws clothes, etc., at Tony and Gordon, expecting them to pack. Tony is alarmed at her ferocity. Gordon starts to pack.

Debs I must be mad thinking this would work, I mean I've tried and it's tough you know bringing up a kid on your own! I was twenty-two when your dad died, they wanted to take you into care, said I couldn't cope, but I said, 'Not on your life, he's my boy and I'm keeping him.' Gordon, can't you even fold up a jumper properly!

She tips the contents of the case which Gordon has been trying to pack on to the floor. He sighs hugely,

*goes to embrace and comfort her, decides against it and
begins repacking the case.*

But make no mistake it's no bloody picnic, never having a
night off and never having enough money and never being
able to see anybody properly because my son is a selfish
little monster and then when I do find a bloke I like, all
right he's not exactly Superman, I mean he wears sandals
and a duffel coat for God's sake, I mean he needs a lot of
work but underneath it all he's basically kind and caring,
he turns out to be the kind of wimp who throws up every
five minutes and takes two and a half hours to find a
runaway kid and I miss your dad!

*The fury evaporates and she is left in tears. Gordon
gently approaches her and strokes her hair. Tony
watches in shocked silence. Eventually Debs and
Gordon kiss. Then Gordon calmly ushers Tony out of
the room. Tony watches as Gordon goes back into the
room, cuddles Debs and switches off the light.*
The hotel room disappears.
*Tony goes up on the balcony above the hotel room
and stares at the moon and the café below.*

Tony After she had started to cry Gordon gave her a
cuddle and I went out. I thought it might be nice for them
to be alone.

*Below, outside the café, a French dog enters and begins
to play a melancholy tune on an accordion.*

The air was fresh and I could hear music and laughter
from the café downstairs . . . And suddenly it all seemed
right, like things had changed and things were different
but somehow I'd changed as well. I couldn't work out
what it was but I thought it probably had something to
do with Josie. And Death-Dealer. And my dad.

Two other dogs enter. One is a female torch singer. The three dogs begin playing boule, a magical game in which the balls make patterns in the air before landing.

And all of a sudden for the first time in ages I got this big lump in my throat and it felt like a cricket ball, it was so big and my eyes felt as wide as moons and without any warning these big hot tears came out, big wet hot tears running down my cheeks like a bathroom tap, and although I didn't make any noise, inside I howled like a dog in the night, and thought about going home.

The dogs notice Tony's tears, and abandon their game to comfort him with a song.

Dogs (*singing*)
    Life
    Is a gay
    Cabaret
    Mon ami
    But there's no
    Guarantee
    Of applause
    Okay
    So you play
    By the rules
    Mon ami
    But it's not quite as simple as boules
    Mon ami
    For fortune makes dogs into fools
    Mon ami
    And 'appiness slips through
    Ze paws
    But if
    You can smile
    Through the tears

Mon ami
Le petit
Victory
Will be yours.

Blackout.
   Curtain.

Act Two

The kitchen set. Six months later.
    Josie is trying to reason with Tony, who is engrossed in Death-Dealer.
Tony *(to the audience)* And when I got up next morning, Josie and her mum and dad had gone. *(to Josie)* Hadn't you?

Josie It wasn't my fault, we got up really early, and I didn't get a chance to say goodbye to you.

Tony Things were different when we got back home. Gordon and Mum were getting on really well and for the first time in years she seemed happy. I waited ages and ages for you to get in touch, but you didn't!

Josie I was ill!

Tony You could easily have written to me!

Josie I got very sick!

Tony I gave you my address!

Josie It wasn't my fault.

Tony Not listening. Go away. I am playing Death-Dealer, I can't hear you.

Josie I couldn't help it, Tony, honestly. I wanted to talk to you but I got really sick, and sometimes when I'm sick I don't know what's happening, or I forget things, or it's just like I'm asleep most of the time!

Tony I'm not listening.

Josie Please, Tony, please listen to me.

Tony You should have called me.

Josie I would have done but I couldn't. I wanted to, I missed you. I thought about you.

Tony Did you?

Josie Yes. I thought about you a lot.

Tony I thought about you. Every time I played Death-Dealer.

Josie It's a good game.

Tony It's even better when you play it with a friend.

Josie Are you ready to play?

Tony Yo!

Josie Are we going to lose?

Tony No!

Josie So stand by your console! Let's go!

Tony Go, go, go! Let's play Death-Dealer!

Josie A story of birth!

Tony And death!

Josie and Tony (*together*) And the bit in between.

Tony (*declaiming*) With a sword called peace and a staff called truth we'll face the sternest task, so debonair and devil may care –

Josie – As he wears the hero's mask –

Tony – If they ask –

Josie – Who is that sturdy man –

Tony – Has he got –

Josie – What it takes –

Tony – To plot and plan –

Josie – Can he win?

Tony – Then I'll grin, of course I can –

Josie – Of course I can –

Josie and Tony (*together*)
Of course I can.
The foot of the mountain
The shore of the sea
The path to the forest
The root of the tree
The silent wizard
The door and its key
The edge of adventure
Is beckoning me
The edge of adventure
Is beckoning me.

Tony The first thing we have to do is work out which level we're at.

Josie Level eighty-three. Now the object of the game is to find out what is in the Basket of Light –

They pull things from out under the sink and act out the game using various props. Celery for the forest, a pan-scrubber for the witch, etc.

– but to get to the Basket of Light you have to go through this huge maze . . .

Tony And escape from the witch –

Josie – and go deep into the forest –

Tony – then get past the geysers of stone . . . into the enchanted fortress –

Josie – facing up to Skullmort the Reaper –

Tony – dodging him and his dragons –

Josie – snatching the Basket of Light out of his hands –

Tony – and then, bring it all the way past Skullmort and his dragons out of the fortress, through the forest, past the geysers of stone and the mirror of the past, out to the threshold, avoiding the poison berries, back on the magic carpet across the stormy sea, back to the mainland and handing over the basket to the Queen, right?

Josie Right!

Tony I'd have liked to have played it with you.

Josie Yeah. So would I.

For a moment it seems as if they might hold hands, but they don't.
  Josie exits.

Tony We never did get a chance to play the game together. 'Cos like I said I never heard from her. I just played it by myself when I got back from France. I played it while Mum and Gordon planned their wedding. I played it during the wedding. I played it all through the honeymoon when they went to Edinburgh and I had to stay with Auntie Lucy. I played it loads and loads and loads of times by myself. And then one night I was in my room and I had just got to an exciting bit when suddenly I heard Mum's voice and she said –

Debs (*off*) Tony!

Tony (*to the audience*) Mum.

Debs Come on, it's tea time.

Tony (*calling off to Debs*) Just five more minutes.

Debs appears at the door. She is heavily pregnant.
During the following Gordon enters and starts cooking
in the kitchen.

Debs Come on love, your tea's ready.

Tony You OK?

Debs Just tired. Your baby brother or sister is obviously
going to be a footballer when they grow up.

Tony What do you mean?

Debs Kicking.

Tony (*listening to the baby*) Weird! You can feel it. (*to
the audience*) Do you want a go? You do, don't you?
Mum, can my friends feel it kicking?

Debs Well, how many of them are there?

Tony About – (*counts the audience*) a million?

Debs No, Tony, I don't mind one or two but I draw the
line at a million.

Tony Grown-ups, eh? No fun. What's for tea?

Debs It's a surprise.

Things are not going terribly well in the kitchen.
Smoke is coming out of various pots and pans.
Eventually, Gordon serves up one portion of sludge.

Tony What is it?

Debs Guess.

Tony Even somebody on *Mastermind* couldn't guess

what that is. Or *Masterchef* (*mimicking Lloyd Grossman*)
'And what can we see through the keyhole this week?' A
plate of gunge. Looks like the stuff Noel Edmonds dumps
on people's heads. Gunge tank, gunge tank!

Debs Eat it up.

Tony It's gunge, isn't it? I mean it's just gunge.

Debs I'm sure it's fine.

Tony Then why aren't you eating it?

Debs I'm not feeling hungry.

Tony Gordon?

Gordon shakes his head.

So you're not hungry either?

Gordon shakes his head.

Brilliant, so I'm the lucky lad who gets to eat all the grey
gunge as served up by Gordon the sludge beast. Gordon
the slop monster.

The telephone rings.

Debs I'll get it. (*She picks up the telephone.*)

Tony I pity the poor baby born into this house! Forced to
eat this muck!

Debs (*speaking into the telephone*) Yes, speaking.

Tony I think it's my duty to warn it! All right, so it's
inside Mum but that means it's only like, four feet away.
It might not be able to see but it must be able to hear
what I'm saying.

Debs Yes, I have a son called Tony. What's he done?

Tony (*directing his whisper at Debs' stomach*) Hallo, baby? Can you hear me, baby?

The Sumo Baby Josie emerges from somewhere on the set.

(*to the Sumo Baby Josie*) Can you hear what I'm saying?

The Baby Josie nods. Throughout the following scene it investigates the kitchen with all the curiosity of the newborn, switching things on, picking things up, etc. Debs and Gordon remain oblivious. Tony clears up any mess the baby makes.

That's your mum, right? You're inside her right now. This is you here.

He pats Debs' bulge. She remains unaware.

Of course being inside you'll never have seen her before. I'll bet you thought she was really glamorous, eh? Well tough, no, that's our mum and we're stuck with her. And this over here is your dad, Gordon. See the resemblance?

The baby is dismayed at the thought that Gordon is its father.

So do you reckon you're daddy's boy or girl? What are you, anyway?

The baby turns its back to the audience and checks its nappy. But it doesn't know whether it's a boy or a girl.

Well whatever you are you're gonna have to eat the rubbish he's cooked.

Debs Who? Josie who? Boulogne?

Tony Boulogne? Is that Josie on the phone?

Debs It's Josie's mum. Eat your supper, Tony, like a good lad.

Tony (*to the baby*) I mean, try it.

The baby tries the food and doesn't like it.

You think that's bad. Wait 'til you see what we had yesterday.

He opens the fridge and takes out three bowls of differently coloured gunge.

That's supposed to be stew, this one's lasagne and that's ratatouille made with real rats. All disgusting. Couldn't taste any worse if you mixed them all together.

The baby does just this.

Debs Gordon, pass me a pencil would you?

Gordon gets up and gives Debs a pencil. The baby makes a huge mess on the table.

Tony Look at all this mess. I'll get the blame for this. (*He places the plate full of multi-coloured gunge on one corner of the table and attempts to clean up.*)

Debs Ward Twelve. Yes, I'll tell him. Yes, I know where it is.

Gordon goes to lean on the table, inadvertently heading straight for the plate of gunge.

Tony (*distracting Gordon*) A wasp! (*He shifts the plate to Gordon's chair.*)

Gordon looks around in horror but can find no wasp. He relaxes and leans against the table.

Sorry, could've sworn I saw a wasp. (*to the baby*) You nearly got me into trouble there. Go on, go back to your womb and stay there.

The baby disappears.

Debs Yes, I'll ask him, but you do understand – Yes, quite . . . All right then, bye.

She replaces the telephone.

That was Josie's mum, remember, the little girl in France. Josie's very ill, she's in hospital and she'd like to see you, but it could be a bit distressing. She's dying, Tony. She hasn't got long left. Do you want to go and see her?

Tony Sure.

Debs (*upset*) Gordon will take you. I'll just get a hankie. (*She exits.*)

Tony Of course I'll go and see her. Just wish it wasn't in hospital that's all. I hate hospitals. I mean the one Dad was in was all right and the people were great but there was nothing they could do. See, the thing is, sometimes there isn't. But yeah, I'll go and see her. But don't you trouble yourself, Gordon.

Gordon is surprised by his friendliness.

You've done an awful lot today. Washed, scrubbed and cooked this lovely supper, you must be exhausted.

Gordon nods appreciatively.

You just sit down and take it easy. (*He takes Gordon by the shoulders and sits him down on the plate of gunge.*) There. That's better isn't it?

The set transforms into a hospital room. There is a telephone next to Josie's bed.
  Gordon and Tony exit.
  Josie is in bed, playing Death-Dealer with her doctor. Josie looks smaller, iller, thinner. The doctor is a full-mask character.

Josie Are you going to do the operation yourself?

The doctor nods.

If it goes wrong will you promise me something?

The doctor nods. She whispers in the doctor's ear.

Promise?

The doctor nods and whispers a question into Josie's ear.

No, he is not my boyfriend! Cheeky rat!

Tony and Gordon enter. Tony has a bunch of flowers.

Tony God, I hate the smell of hospitals . . .

The doctor ushers Gordon and Tony in. Gordon hangs back while Tony approaches the bed. He and Josie are rather shy in each other's presence.

Hi.

Josie Hi.

Tony Flowers.

Josie Nice.

Tony For you.

Josie Ta.

Tony But don't get the wrong idea. It's not like I'm your boyfriend or anything.

Josie No. Can you put these in some water please, Doctor? And stop laughing!

The doctor takes the flowers and exits.

Tony How you doing?

Josie All right.

Tony Right.

Josie How you doing?

Tony All right.

Josie Right.

Tony You look thinner.

Josie You look fatter.

Tony You look balder.

Josie You look hairier. Hi, Gordon.

Tony Say Hi, Gordon!

Gordon waves shyly.

Tony He's shy. He's a wally.

Josie He's nice. You're nice, Gordon.

Gordon is pleased.

Take your duffel off.

Gordon removes his duffel and looks for somewhere to hang it. He almost hangs it on Josie's drip-feeder but realizes that might be a mistake.

Tony He must really like you. He hardly ever takes his duffel off in public. I'm beginning to think he's not a man at all, he's Paddington Bear trying to live quietly under an assumed name.

Josie Has he married your mum yet?

Tony Yeah. Ages ago.

Josie Good wedding?

Tony No.

Josie Why not?

Tony I had to wear a suit.

Josie Ha ha! I bet you looked like a monkey!

Tony No I didn't.

Gordon nods.

Well actually, yes, I did.

Josie Has she had the baby yet?

Tony Any minute now.

Josie You excited, Gordon?

Gordon gives a bad impression of someone with nerves of steel.

Boy or girl?

Tony Don't know.

Josie They can tell. Scans.

Tony She doesn't want to know. Won't have one. She's had lots of rows with the doctors. So. Why didn't you come and see me after Boulogne?

Josie Regression.

Tony What does that mean?

Josie I got worse.

Tony How bad?

Josie They're going to operate. Find out. But it looks bad.

Tony Are you going to die?

Gordon is alarmed by this but Josie is calm.

Josie I might, I might not. Who knows? I'll fight. I might win, I might lose.

Tony What – what happens when you die?

Josie Good question. I don't know.

Tony When my dad died –

Josie Yeah?

Tony I think he turned into a bell. On the moon. But a really high-pitched bell, so high nobody but dogs can hear it.

Josie A bell?

Tony A bell.

Josie Do you think it's true?

Tony It's true if I believe it.

Josie Do you believe it?

Tony I don't know. (*to the audience*) And then something really strange happened.

Josie A bell. I like that. I like the sound of a bell.

A telephone rings. The noise startles Gordon.

Tony Gordon, the phone's ringing.

The coincidence has frightened Gordon.

Come on, get it together! Answer the phone!

Eventually Gordon answers the telephone. He does not react at first but then he panics and puts the phone down, stunned.

Mum?

Gordon nods.

Josie The baby?

Gordon nods.

You're going to be a daddy!

Gordon nods.

Tony Well don't just stand there, go!

Gordon runs off. Then he runs back on to look for his duffel, bumping into things as he does so. Eventually, after a tussle, he finds the coat, and runs off.

Josie and Tony are left alone. There is an awkward silence.

Josie I cracked Death-Dealer.

Tony You've done it?

Josie Once.

Tony Once is enough! Well, wicked! So you've actually looked into the Basket of Light?

Josie Maybe.

Tony And you know what's in there?

Josie Might do.

Tony So are you going to tell me what it is?

Josie Possibly.

Tony When?

Josie After the operation.

The doctor enters.

Oh oh. Time to go. I know the drill, don't worry.

The doctor removes the drip from Josie's arm.

I'm scared.

Tony Eh.

Josie I'm scared, Tony.

Tony Nothing to be scared of, right.

Josie It's an adventure, right?

Tony Right. Just . . . it's the beginning of the game, right. On to the magic carpet.

Josie Goodbye, Tony.

Tony See you later.

Josie Maybe.

The doctor wheels Josie off. Tony is left alone.

Tony I just wait here, do I? I said I just wait here. Do I? Hallo? What do I do? What do I do? (*to the audience*) There was only one thing I could do. (*He picks up Death-Dealer.*) One last try, Death-Dealer. Level one hundred!

The set transforms into the Death-Dealer landscape. A heart monitor effect gives us an eerie percussion. A giant projection shows us Josie's heartbeat.

Here we stand on the threshold of the forest. (*He calls.*) Josie, Josie, where are you?

Josie appears.

Are you ready to play?

Josie Yo.

Tony Are you going to lose?

Josie No.

Tony and Josie (*together*) Let's go.

Tony First we just stare into the mirror and learn the truth of the past.

Josie Right, the truth is this, your dad died aged thirty-one, these things happen, life goes on.

Tony And so does death! Next step?

Josie Escaping from the witch, easy, jump three steps –

> *They do.*

– and then produce the sword called 'Peace' and the staff called 'Truth'.

> *The sword and staff appear magically.*

Tony Then enter the forest to face Skullmort the Reaper.

Josie But beware. The forest floor contains ten geysers which will turn you to stone if you step upon them. Right, let's see who goes first. (*She uses the chancer to decide.*) Your full name this time.

Tony T.O.N.Y. M.A.S.O.N.

Josie Oh oh. It says I'm first.

Tony Test the way with the staff of truth . . . see and be careful!

> *He reaches out with the staff and touches the floor. A geyser of steam shoots up into the air.*

Josie Wish me luck.

Tony You'll need it!

*Josie crosses the geyser field, obeying Tony's
instructions as he plays the game.*

Right . . . left . . . careful . . . left . . .

*Josie feels her way with the staff. The geysers explode
all around her but she reaches the next section
unharmed. A figure (Skullmort the Reaper) begins to
grow. A bridge forms between Josie and him. As the
tension mounts the beat of the heart monitor quickens.
Eventually Josie traverses the floor and successfully
reaches the bridge.*

She's done it. Hooray!

Josie I am here, I am ready. Where is Skullmort the
Reaper?

Skullmort appears. He is huge and threatening.

Tony Go on, go on. What are you waiting for? Kill him!

Josie I can't.

Tony Why not?

Josie I'm not strong enough. I just have to face him as
best I can. I can spit, I can scream, I can cry, but I can't
change it.

Tony But how are you going to get the basket?

Josie I'll have to take my chances . . .

*She crosses the bridge and is absorbed by Skullmort
and his darkness. Then from within him comes a
powerful light. We see her clasping a basket in her
arms. Tony is screaming at her to leave but she is
enthralled. The light grows mighty and Skullmort
recedes. Now, she is ablaze with whiteness.*

Tony Josie!

He tries to cross but the geysers stop him.

Josie! Don't die!

Then, suddenly, Josie is gone. The heart monitor effect is stilled and the set reforms into Tony's house. Tony is alone in half light.

You can't die! You can't leave me! It's a terrible feeling to be left behind, like when Dad died, it's like being abandoned. What about me? What about me? No, it's not fair, it's not fair! What about me? (*He falls to his knees exhausted, crying.*)

Debs enters.

Debs Hey, hey, hey . . .

Tony The game isn't fair. (*He throws Death-Dealer away.*)

Debs Life never is. Or death.

Tony I don't want to play any more.

Debs You will. There's so much to do. You have to help. It's not just me and you and Gordon now.

Tony Why did she have to die?

Debs We all have to die. But life goes on. And she left you a present.

Tony What present?

Debs Josie told the doctor how the game ends. She wanted you to know. Look . . .

Gordon enters carrying a basket. Light comes from it.

Tony The Silent Wizard. It all makes sense. The Silent

Wizard rescues the basket? Right?

Gordon nods.

And the hero opens the basket to find what's inside. Right? (*He takes the basket from Gordon.*)

Gordon exits.

Debs Right.

Tony And we all want to know what's inside the basket, right? Well the answer is –

The baby appears.

– a baby. Josie two. Josie the sequel. Which is where the story started. Say hallo, everybody. Say hallo, Josie.

The baby throws up.

Charming. Well, a little bit of sick –

Debs Never hurt anyone. And she is a bit excited.

Tony Well she would be. It is a special day.

Debs takes the baby.
Gordon enters with a birthday cake, lit with one candle.

Now. Everyone sing very quietly.

He leads the audience in singing 'Happy Birthday to Josie'. She blows the candle out. Tony gives her three cheers.

One year old.

Debs One year to the day since Josie died.

Tony A life taken.

Debs A life given.

Tony A new life for me and Mum and stupid old gormless Gordon.

Gordon looks sad and goes to exit.

Except Gordon turned out to be anything but gormless.

Gordon stops in his tracks.

Because he loves my mum and Josie and in a certain way, a sneaky sort of way, a sneaky grown-up sort of way he loves me. And in a sort of way, a sneaky sort of way . . . I love him.

He cuddles Gordon, who is stunned but delighted and cuddles him back.
Gordon and Debs exit with Baby Josie.

I even put up with the latest present he bought me. You're not gonna believe this. (*He whistles.*)

A dog appears and leaps on him, humping his leg.

A dog for me to look after. Well, what with feeding it and taking it for a walk and trying to stop it spending its whole life sniffing other dogs' bums then licking me on the lips, it's a full-time job. And then of course looking after baby Josie and Mum and keeping Gordon out of trouble, you can see I've got my hands full.

He throws a bone for his dog. It barks.
The pack of dogs enters.

That's it . . . fetch. Fetch. Good dogs!

They chase each other around before coming to rest at Tony's feet in a pile.

By the end of the day I'm absolutely exhausted. I get into bed and Gordon reads me stories before I go to sleep, of dragons and monsters and heroes and death and life. And

I drift off thinking big thoughts, important grown-up thoughts, knowing that however long we get a chance to live it, life is wonderful. Tonight, when you're in bed, think about that. But just before you drift off, when you're on the edge of sleep, just do me one last favour. Smile, think about the moon . . . and listen.

> *Tony and the dogs howl at the moon. The moon responds with the sound of bells. Tinkling at first, then more clamorous, until the night is alive with their chimes.*
> *Blackout.*
> *Curtain.*

Children's Theatre Companies

Action Transport Theatre Company,
Whitby Hall, Stanney Lane, Ellesmere Port, South Wirral,
L65 9AE. *Tel:* 0151 357 2120; *fax:* 0151 356 4057.
Contact: Paula Davenport Ball, General Manager.

Arad Goch,
Stryd Y Baddon, Aberystwyth, Dyfed, SY23 2NN.
Tel: 01970 617998; *fax:* 01970 611223.
Contact: Jeremy Turner, Artistic Director.

ARC Theatre Ensemble,
Eastbury Manor House, Eastbury Square, Barking, Essex, IG11 5SN.
Tel: 0181 594 1095; *fax:* 0181 594 1052.
Contact: Nita Bocking, Administrator.

B.A.C.,
Lavender Hill, Battersea, London, SW11 5TF. *Tel:* 0171 223 6557/
325 8206; *fax:* 0171 978 5207; *e-mail:* marketing@bac.org.uk.
Contact: Slavka Jovanovic, Education Officer.

Baboro Galway International Children's Festival,
Black Box, Dyke Road, Galway, Ireland. *Tel:* 353 91 562594;
fax: 353 91 562655; *e-mail:* gaf@iol.ie.
Contact: Jean Parkinson, Executive Director.

Barking Dog Theatre Company,
Room 49, Millmead Business Centre, Millmead Road, Tottenham
Hale, London, N17 9QU. *Tel:* 0181 880 9977; *fax:* 0181 880 9978;
e-mail: pat@bdog.co.uk.
Contact: Patrick Jacobs, Director.

Belgrade Theatre,
Belgrade Square, Coventry, CV1 1GS. *Tel:* 01203 256431;
fax: 01203 550680; *e-mail:* mnpegg@globalnet.co.uk.
Contact: Matthew Pegg, Head of Young People's Work.

Birmingham Repertory Theatre,
Broad Street, Birmingham, B1 2EP. *Tel:* 0121 245 2000;
fax: 0121 245 2100; *e-mail:* rachel.gartside@birmingham-rep.com.
Contact: Rachel Gartside, Head of Education.

Blue Boat,
2/3 4 Hermitage Park, Edinburgh, *Tel:* 07041 323046/
0131 554 6335; *e-mail:* blueboats@hotmail.com.
Contact: Mark Pencak, Director.

Booster Cushion Theatre,
Building B, 1st Floor, Chocolate Factory, Clarendon Road,
London, N22 6XJ. *Tel:* 0181 888 4545; *fax:* 0181 365 8686.
Contact: Philip Sherman, Performer/Director.

Bournemouth Theatre in Education,
BCCA, 93 Haviland Road, Bournemouth, BH7 6HJ.
Tel: 01202 395759; *fax:* 01202 399597;
e-mail: bcca@bournemouth.gov.uk.
Contact: Tony Horitz, Team Leader.

Bruvvers Theatre Company,
Ouseburn Warehouse Workshops, 36 Lime Street, Ouseburn,
Newcastle-Upon-Tyne, NE1 2PQ. *Tel:* 0191 261 9230;
fax: 0191 261 923.
Contact: Michael Mould, Director.

C & T,
University College Worcester, Henwick Grove, Worcester, WR2
6AJ. *Tel:* 01905 855436; *fax:* 01905 855132; *e-mail:*
CandT@worc.ac.uk.
Contact: Jack Shuttleworth, Director.

Cambridge City Council Leisure Services,
Leisure Services, Cambridge City Council, The Guildhall,
Cambridge, CB2 3QJ. *Tel:* 01223 457514; *fax:* 01223 457529;
e-mail: francesca@cambridge.gov.uk.
Contact: Frances Alderton, Promotions Assistant.

Chichester Festival Theatre,
Oaklands Park, Chichester, W. Sussex, PO19 4AP.
Tel: 01243 784437; *fax:* 01243 787288; *e-mail:* educ@cft.org.uk.
Contact: Andy Brereton, Education Director.

Classworks Theatre,
Cambridge Drama Centre, Covent Garden, Cambridge, CB1 2HR.
Tel: 01223 461901; *fax:* 01223 518176.
Contact: Kathryn Lawrence.

Cleveland Theatre Company,
Arts Centre, Vane Terrace, Darlington, DL3 7AX.
Tel: 01325 352 004; *fax:* 01325 369 404;
e-mail: ctc@clevelandtheatre.demon.co.uk.
Contact: Paul Harman, Artistic Director.

Clown Fizzie Lizzie,
41 Eastlake House, Frampton Street, London, NW8 8LU.
Tel: 0171 723 3877; *fax:* 0171 723 3877;
e-mail: clownfizzielizzie@ukbusiness.com.
Contact: Elizabeth Morgan.

Contact Theatre,
Oxford Road, Manchester, M15 6JA. *Tel:* 0161 274 3434;
fax: 0161 273 6286.
Contact: Lisa Dryburgh, Head of Marketing.

Cornelius and Jones Productions,
49 Carters Close, Sherington, Newport Pagnell, MK16 9NW.
Tel: 01908 612593; *fax:* 01908 216400;
e-mail: pa@boom.demon.co.uk.
Contact: Sue Leech, Co-Director.

Crucible Theatre In Education,
Crucible Theatre, 55 Norfolk Street, Sheffield, S. Yorks., S1 1DA.
Tel: 0114 249 5999; *fax:* 0114 249 6003.
Contact: Amanda J. Smith, Director.

Cwmni'r Fran Wen,
The Old Primary School, Pentraeth Road, Menai Bridge, Anglesey,
LL59 5HS. *Tel:* 01248 715048; *fax:* 01248 715225.
Contact: Medwen Davies, Administrator.

Dr Palfi – Consultant Laughologist,
5 Kingsmead, Wickham, Hants, PO17 5AU; *fax:* 01329 832695.
Contact: H.P. Rinehart, Artistic Director/Performer.

Freehand Theatre,
1 Reynard Villas, Mayfield Grove, Baildon, Shipley, W. Yorks.,
BD17 6DY. *Tel:* 01274 585277; *fax:* 01274 585277;
e-mail: freehand@pop 3.poptel.org.uk.
Contact: Lizzie Allen, Co-Director.

Futures Theatre Company,
44 Clarence Avenue, London, SW4 8JA. *Tel:* 0181 671 1200;
fax: 0181 674 8142.
Contact: Caroline Bryant.

Giant Productions,
7 Water Row, Govan, Glasgow, G51 3UW. *Tel:* 0141 445 6000;
fax: 0141 445 4446.
Contact: Phyllis Steel, Director.

Greenwich & Lewisham Young Peoples Theatre,
Burrage Road Plumstead, London, SE18 7JZ. *Tel:* 0181 854 1316;
fax: 0181 317 8595.
Contact: Viv Harris, Artistic & Education.

Half Moon Young People's Theatre,
43 Whitehorse Road, Stepney, London, E1 0ND.
Tel: 0171 265 8138; *fax:* 0171 702 7220;
e-mail: halfmoon@dircon.co.uk.
Contact: Chris Elwell, Artistic Director.

Hand to Mouth,
51 Arnold Road, Southampton, SO17 1TF. *Tel:* 01703 555392;
fax: 01703 555392; *e-mail:* martsu@btinternet.com.
Contact: Martin Bridle, Director.

Haymarket Theatre Outreach Department,
Belgrave Gate, Leicester, LE1 3YQ. *Tel:* 0116 2530021;
fax: 0116 2513310; *e-mail:* outreach@haymarket.u-net.com
Contact: Ellen Bianchin, Education Administrator.

Interplay Theatre Company,
Armley Ridge Road, Leeds, W. Yorks., LS12 3LE.
Tel: 0113 263 8556; *fax:* 0113 231 9285;
e-mail: interplay@pop3.poptel.org.uk.
Contact: Gemma Kelmanson, Administrator.

Jack Drum Arts & Entertainment,
West New Houses, Baldersdale, Barnard Castle, County Durham,
DL12 9UU. *Tel:* 01833 650623; *fax:* 01833 650623.
Contact: Julie Ward, Partner.

Kaleidoscope Children's Festival,
Old Lynturk Church, Muir of Fowlis, Nr Alford, Aberdeenshire,
AB33 8HS. *Tel:* 019755 81258; *fax:* 019755 81474.
Contact: Linda Lees Hislop, General Manager.

Kazzum Arts Project,
BAC, Lavender Hill, London, SW11 5TF. *Tel:* 0171 223 0703;
fax: 0171 223 0776; *e-mail:* kazzum@compuserve.com
Contact: Felicity White, Education Officer.

Komedia,
45–47 Gardner Street, Brighton, E. Sussex, BN1 1UN.
Tel: 01273 647101; *fax:* 01273 647102;
e-mail: pippa@komedia.dircon.co.uk.
Contact: Pippa Edwards, Education Officer.

Krazy Kat Theatre Company,
173 Hartington Road, Brighton, E. Sussex, BN2 3PA. *Tel:* 01273
692552; *fax:* 01273 692552; *e-mail:* kkat@kkat.deon.co.uk.
Contact: Alistair Macmillan, Co-Artistic Director.

Lambeth Children's Theatre Co,
27 Wingmore Road, London,
SE24 0AS. *Tel:* 0171 733 5270; *fax:* 0171 326 0146.
Contact: Raymond Cook, Director.

Lantern Theatre Company,
16 Claudian Place, St Albans, Herts, AL3 4JE. *Tel:* 01727 761007; *fax:* 01727 761007; *e-mail:* lantern@dircon. co.uk.
Contact: Tony Peters, Director.

Leap Confronting Conflict,
8 Lennox Road, London, N4 3NW. *Tel:* 0171 272 5630; *fax:* 0171 272 8405.
Contact: Tess Walsh, Administrator.

London Drama,
Central School of Speech & Drama, Eton Avenue, London, NW3 3HY. *Tel:* 0171 722 4730; *e-mail:* Londrama@aol.com
Contact: Chris Lawrence.

London International Festival of Theatre,
19/20 Great Sutton Street, London, EC1V 0DR.
Tel: 0171 490 3964/5; *fax:* 0171 490 3976;
e-mail: left@easynet.co.uk.
Contact: Tony Fegan, Education Director.

London Workshop Company,
Chiswick Town Hall, Heathfield Terrace, London, W4 4JE.
Tel: 0181 996 9085; *fax:* 0181 996 9085;
e-mail: londonworkshop@compuserve.com
Contact: Ruth Burgess, Director.

Ludus Dance Agency,
Assembly Rooms, King Street, Lancaster, LA1 1RE.
Tel: 01524 35936; *fax:* 01524 847744; *e-mail:* ludus@easynet.org
Contact: Jacqueline Greaves, Head of Touring.

Lynx Theatre in Education,
13 Tunn Street, Fakeham, Norfolk, NR21 9BJ. *Tel:* 01328 864958; *fax:* 01328 864958.
Contact: Lynne Kentish, Director.

M6 Theatre Company,
Hamer C.P. School, Albert Royds Street, Rochdale, Lancs.,
OL16 2SU. *Tel:* 01706 355898; *fax:* 01706 711700;
e-mail: info@m6theatre.freeserve.co.uk.
Contact: Jane Milne, Administrator.

MAC,
Cannon Hill Park, Birmingham, B12 9QH. *Tel:* 0121 440 4221;
fax: 0121 446 4372; *e-mail:* mac.birmingham@btinternet.com
Contact: Dorothy Wilson, Director.

Magic Carpet Theatre,
18 Church Street, Sutton-On-Hull, East Riding, HU7 4TS.
Tel: 01482 709939; *fax:* 01482 787362;
e-mail: jon@magiccarpet.demon.co.uk.
Contact: Jon Marshall, Director.

Man Mela Theatre Company,
The Albany, Douglas Way, Deptford, London, SE8 4AG.
Tel: 0181 691 3277 x 117; *fax:* 0181 469 2253.
Contact: Caroline Goffin, Administrator.

Mercury Theatre,
Balkerne Gate, Colchester, Essex, C01 1PT. *Tel:* 01206 577006;
fax: 01206 769607.
Contact: Adrian Stokes, Associate Director.

Merseyside Young People's Theatre Company,
13 Hope Street, Liverpool, L1 9BH. *Tel:* 0151 708 0877;
fax: 0151 707 9950; *e-mail:* MYPT@uk.com.
Contact: Karen O'Donnell, Administrator.

Mimika Theatre,
26 Highbury Terrace, Leeds, W. Yorks., LS6 4ET.
Tel: 0113 2740053; *fax:* 0113 2740053;
e-mail: mimika@btinternet.com
Contact: Jenny Ward, Performer/Administrator.

Miskin Theatre,
North West Kent College, Miskin Road, Dartford, Kent, DA1 2LU.
Tel: 01322 629433; *fax:* 01322 629469.
Contact: Laurajane Lavender, Administrator.

Movingstage Marionette Company,
78 Middleton Road, London, E8 4BP. *Tel:* 0171 249 6876;
fax: 0171 683 0741; *e-mail:* puppet@mcmail.com.
Contact: Juliet Middleton, Co-Director.

Oily Cart,
Smallwood School Annexe, Smallwood Road, Tooting,
London SW17 0TW. *Tel:* 0181 672 6329; *fax:* 0181 672 0792;
e-mail: oilycart@premier.co.uk.
Contact: Joanna Ridout, General Manager.

Old Town Hall Theatre,
High Street, Hemel Hempstead, Herts, HP1 3AE. *Tel:* 01442
228098; *fax:* 01442 234072; *e-mail:* oldtownhall@dial.pipex.com.
Contact: Sherrell Perkin, Education Officer.

Padgate Recreation Centre,
Insall Road, Padgate, Warrington, WA2 0HD. *Tel:* 01925 815069;
fax: 01925 816366.
Contact: Jackie Moore, Centre Manager.

Palace Theatre,
Education Department, Clarendon Road, Watford, WD1 1JZ.
Tel: 01923 235455; *fax:* 01923 819664;
e-mail: education@watfordtheatre.co.uk.
Contact: Hassina Khan, Education Manager.

Parasol Theatre,
Garden House, 4 Sunnyside, Wimbledon, London, SW19 4SL.
Tel: 0181 946 9478; *fax:* 0181 946 0228.
Contact: Richard Gill, Artistic Director.

Pied Piper Company,
1 Lilian Place, Coxcombe Lane, Chiddingfold, Surrey, GU8 4QA.
Tel: 01428 684022; *fax:* 01428 684022.
Contact: Tina Williams, Artistic Director.

Pilot Theatre Company,
Glass Houghton Cultural Centre, Redhill Avenue, Castleford,
W. Yorks., WF10 4QH. *Tel:* 01977 604852; *fax:* 01977 512819;
e-mail: pilot.theatre@geo2.poptel.org.uk.
Contact: Veronica Bailey, Administrative Director.

Playtime Theatre Company,
18 Bennell's Avenue, Whitstable, Kent, Ct5 2HP.
Tel: 01227 266272; *fax:* 01227 266272;
e-mail: playtime@dircon.co.uk.
Contact: Sara Kettlewell, Director.

Polka Theatre For Children,
240 The Broadway, Wimbledon, London SW19 1SB.
Tel: 0181 542 4258; *fax:* 0181 542 7723;
e-mail: polkatheatre@dial.pipex.com.
Contact: Vicky Ireland, Artistic Director.

Pop-Up Theatre,
404 St John Street, London, EC1V 4NJ. *Tel:* 0171 837 7588;
fax: 0171 837 7599; *e-mail:* popup@dircon.co.uk.
Contact: Jackie Eley, Administrative Director.

Proper Job Theatre Projects,
48A Byram Arcade, Westgate, Huddersfield, W. Yorks., HD1 1ND.
Tel: 01484 514687; *fax:* 01484 424403;
e-mail: proper-job@geo2.poptel.org.uk.
Contact: Rhian Jones, Administrator.

Proteus Theatre Company,
Fairfield Arts Centre, Council Road, Basingstoke, Hants,
RG21 3DH. *Tel:* 01256 354541; *fax:* 01256 356186;
e-mail: proteus@dircon.co.uk.
Contact: Jason Knight, Administrator.

Quicksilver Theatre,
4 Enfield Road, London, N1 5AZ. *Tel:* 0171 241 2942;
fax: 0171 254 3119; *e-mail:* qsilver@easynet.co.uk.
Contact: Helen Gethin, Administrator.

Red Ladder Theatre Company,
3 St. Peter's Buildings, York Street, Leeds, W. Yorks., LS9 8AJ.
Tel: 0113 2455311; *fax:* 0113 2455351;
e-mail: red-ladder@geo2.poptel.org.uk.
Contact: Janis Smyth, Company Administrator.

Roundabout Theatre in Education,
Nottingham Playhouse, Wellington Circus, Nottingham, NG1 5AF.
Tel: 0115 947 4361; *fax:* 0115 953 9055;
e-mail: roundabout@org.uk.
Contact: Andrew Breakwell, Artistic Director.

Royal Lyceum Theatre,
Grindlay Street, Edinburgh, EH3 9AX. *Tel:* 0131 229 7404;
fax: 0131 228 3955.
Contact: Steven Small, Education Development Officer.

Sacred Earth Drama Trust,
3 Vernon Street, Old Trafford, Manchester, M16 9JP.
Tel: 0161 226 8127.
Contact: Gordon MacLellan, Administrator.

Salamander Theatre,
333 Chiswick High Road, London, W4 4HS.
Tel: 0181 994 4969; *fax:* 0181 742 3923;
e-mail: salamander.theatre@btinternet.co.
Contact: Tom Morris, Company Administrator.

SCAT Theatre Company,
Portsmouth Arts Centre, Reginald Road, Portsmouth, PO4 9HN.
Tel: 01705 826592.
Contact: Paul Hayles, Co-Director.

Scottish International Children's Festival,
5th Floor, 45A George Street, Edinburgh, EH2 2HT.
Tel: 0131 225 8050; *fax:* 0131 225 6440;
e-mail: tony@sicf.ednet.co.uk.
Contact: Tony Reekie, Director.

Sixth Sense,
c/o Swindon College, Regent Circus, Swindon, SN1 1PT. *Tel:*
01793 614864; *fax:* 01793 616715; *e-mail:* sstc@dircon.co.uk.
Contact: Victoria Wicks, Company Administrator.

Small World Theatre,
Fern Villa, Llandygwydd, Cardigan, Ceredigion, SA43 2QX.
Tel: 01239 682785; *fax:* 01239 682785;
e-mail: smallworld@enterprise.net.
Contact: Ann Shrosbree.

SNAP Theatre Company,
2 The Causeway, Bishop's Stortford, Herts CM23 2EJ.
Tel: 01279 836 2000; *fax:* 01279 501 472.
Contact: David Padgett, Administrator.

Spotlites Theatre Company,
King's Theatre, 338 High Street, Chatham, Kent, ME4 4NR.
Tel: 01634 829468; *fax:* 01634 403737;
e-mail: spotlites@hotmail.com.
Contact: Rachel King, Artistic Director.

Stephen Baron's Piano Music Theatre,
160 Victoria Road, London, N22 7XQ. *Tel:* 0181 888 6536;
fax: 0181 888 6536. *Contact:* Stephen Baron, Director.

Storybox Theatre,
1 Bishops Road, Cleeve, Bristol, BS49 4NQ. *Tel:* 01934 833575;
fax: 01934 833575.
Contact: Tanya Landman, Co-Director.

T.I.E.
Tours, PO Box 25331, London, NW5 4ZG. *Tel:* 0171 688 1972;
e-mail: andii@globalnet.co.uk.
Contact: Andy Hickson.

TAG Theatre Company,
18 Albion Street, Glasgow, G1 1LH. *Tel:* 0141 552 4949;
fax: 0141 552 0666; *e-mail:* tag@glasgow.almac.co.uk.
Contact: Jon Morgan, General Manager.

Take Art!,
Unit 10, North Street Workshops, Stoke-Sub-Hamdon, Somerset,
TA14 6QR. *Tel:* 01935 823151; *fax:* 01935 823102;
e-mail: takeart@dial.pipex.com.
Contact: Ralph Lister, Director.

Tam Tam Theatre,
145 Pepys Road, New Cross, London, SE14 5SG. *Tel:* 0171 277
5874; *fax:* 0171 277 5874.
Contact: Marleen Vermeulen, Artistic Director.

Theatr Iolo,
Old School Building, Cefn Road, Mynachdy, Cardiff, CF4 3HS.
Tel: 01222 613782; *fax:* 01222 520786.
Contact: Gillian Dale.

Theatr Powys,
Drama Centre, Tremont Road, Llandrindod Wells, LD1 5EB.
Tel: 01597 824444; *fax:* 01597 824381.
Contact: Nikki Leopold, General Manager.

Theatre Centre,
Toynbee Workshops, 3 Gunthorpe Street, London, E1 7RQ.
Tel: 0171 377 0379; *fax:* 0171 377 1376; *e-mail:* theacen@aol.com.
Contact: Brenda Murphy, Education Officer.

Theatre Company Blah, Blah, Blah!,
East Leeds Family Learning Centre, Brooklands View, Seacroft,
Leeds, W. Yorks., LS14 6SA. *Tel:* 0113 224 3171; *fax:* 0113 224
3685; *e-mail:* blahblahblah@pop3.poptel.org.uk.
Contact: Anthony Haddon.

Theatre Venture,
The Resources Centre, Stratford, Leywick Street, London, E15
3DD. *Tel:* 0181 519 6678; *fax:* 0181 519 8769; *e-mail:*
info@theatre-venture.org.
Contact: Rosemary Evans, Administrator.

Theatre-rites,
23 Windsor Road, London, N7 6JG. *Tel:* 0171 686 0771;
fax: 0171 686 0771; *e-mail:* info@theatre-rites.demon.co.uk.
Contact: Penny Bernand, Artistic Director.

Tiebreak Theatre Company,
Heartsease High School, Marryat Road, Norwich, NR7 9DF.
Tel: 01603 435209; *fax:* 01603 435184;
e-mail: tie.break@virgin.net.
Contact: Anne Giles, Administrator.

Travelling Light Theatre Company,
St George Community School, Russell Town Avenue, Bristol,
BS5 9JH. *Tel:* 0117 955 0086; *fax:* 0117 941 3557;
e-mail: admin@travlight.co.uk.
Contact: Jude Merrill, Artistic Producer.

Tutti Frutti,
2 Wells Croft, Meanwood, Leeds, LS6 4LA. *Tel:* 0113 278 3307;
fax: 0113 225 9055; *e-mail:* niladri.axis@dial.pipex.com.
Contact: Niladri, Director.

Unicorn Arts Theatre,
St Mark's Studios, Chillingworth Road, London N7 8QJ.
Tel: 0171 700 0702; *fax:* 0171 700 387.
Contact: Tony Graham, Artistic Director.

Visible Fictions,
Royal Lyceum Theatre, 30b Grindlay Street, Edinburgh, EH3 9AX.
Tel: 0131 229 7404 x2137; *fax:* 0131 228 3955.
Contact: The Administrator.

Walk The Plank,
1, The Quays, Salford, M5 2SQ. *Tel:* 0161 873 7350;
fax: 0161 848 0892; *e-mail:* liz.pugh@mcr1.poptel.org.uk.
Contact: Liz Pugh, Producer.

Warwick Arts Centre,
University of Warwick, Coventry, CV4 7AL. *Tel:* 01203 524252/
523734; *fax:* 01203 523883;
e-mail: b.c.bishop@warwick.ac.uk.
Contact: Brian Bishop, Education Liaison Officer.

Watermans Arts Centre,
40 High Street, Brentford, Middlesex, TW8 0QU.
Tel: 0181 847 5651; *fax:* 0181 569 8592.
Contact: Tim Jones, Arts Education Programmer.

West Yorkshire Playhouse,
Playhouse Square, Quarry Hill, Leeds, W. Yorks., LS2 7UP.
Tel: 0113 2442141; *fax:* 0113 2448252.
Contact: Gail McIntyre, Director, Schools Company.

Y Touring,
10 Lennox Road, Finsbury Park, London, N4 3NW.
Tel: 0171 272 5755; *fax:* 0171 272 8413;
e-mail: ytouring@ytouring.demon.co.uk.
Contact: Nigel Townsend, Artistic Director.

Young Vic,
66 The Cut, London, SE1 8LZ. Tel: 0171 633 0133;
fax: 0171 928 1585.
Contact: Sue Emmas, Artistic Associate.